PREFACE

China's arms transfers have become the focus of considerable attention. In the 1980s, China emerged as a major supplier of conventional weapons to the developing world. More recently, China's transfers of ballistic missiles and nuclear weapons technology, as well as equipment and materials that could be used in the manufacture of chemical and biological weapons, have seized world attention, particularly in the United States. This study documents China's principal arms-transfer relationships, analyzes the motivations of supplier and recipients, evaluates which arms transfers are of greatest concern, and identifies possible constraints on China's arms sales. It then assesses the threat posed by the transfers.

This study is part of a larger, multiyear project on "Chinese Defense Modernization and Its Implications for the U.S. Air Force." Other reports from this project include:

- Mark Burles, *Chinese Policy Toward Russia and the Central Asian Republics*, MR-1045-AF, 1999.

- Zalmay Khalilzad, Abram Shulsky, Daniel Byman, Roger Cliff, David Orletsky, David Shlapak, and Ashley Tellis, *The United States and a Rising China: Strategic and Military Implications*, MR-1082-AF, 1999.

This project is conducted in the Strategy and Doctrine Program of Project AIR FORCE under the sponsorship of the Deputy Chief of Staff for Air and Space Operations, U.S. Air Force (AF/XO). Comments are welcome and may be directed either to the authors or the project leader, Dr. Zalmay Khalilzad.

PROJECT AIR FORCE

Project AIR FORCE, a division of RAND, is the Air Force federally funded research and development center (FFRDC) for studies and analysis. It provides the Air Force with independent analysis of policy alternatives affecting the development, employment, combat readiness, and support of current and future aerospace forces. Research is performed in four programs: Aerospace Force Development; Manpower, Personnel, and Training; Research Management; and Strategy and Doctrine.

Project AIR FORCE

CHINA'S ARMS SALES

MOTIVATIONS AND IMPLICATIONS

DANIEL L. BYMAN
ROGER CLIFF

Prepared for the
UNITED STATES AIR FORCE

RAND

CONTENTS

China's arms sales pose a moderate threat to U.S. interests. Beijing has sold arms to leading rogue states, such as Iran and Iraq, and has transferred technology related to nuclear, biological, and chemical (NBC) weapons and their associated delivery systems. Through China's help, states such as Iran have developed their own defense industrial base, making them more autonomous and threatening to U.S. allies. Although Chinese sales have fallen in recent years, and Beijing has become more responsible regarding the sale of NBC technologies and missile systems, further progress is necessary to stop China's behavior from posing a threat to U.S. interests.

China emerged as a major source of arms transfers in the 1980s, and by 1987 was the world's fourth largest seller of conventional arms. However, Chinese weapon sales diminished sharply after the end of the Iran-Iraq war in 1988, and demand for Chinese weapons fell further after Operation Desert Storm dramatically demonstrated the superiority of Western high-tech weaponry over low-tech Chinese and Soviet systems. The growing availability of cheap—and more advanced—Russian weapons also reduced demand for Chinese weapons.

As China's conventional weapon sales began to taper off, it began transferring systems and technology that were much more worrisome: those associated with missiles and NBC weapons. The decisions to engage in such transfers had been made well before the slump in the demand for Chinese conventional arms, but these transactions did not begin to receive public attention until the late 1980s. In 1988, U.S. intelligence revealed that China had sold nuclear-capable intermediate-range ballistic missiles to Saudi Arabia. This was followed by reports that China was assisting ballistic missile programs in Iran and Pakistan. Even more alarming was China's assistance to several countries' NBC programs. The most extensive assistance was to Pakistan, where China apparently provided Islamabad with both a nuclear weapon design and fissile material. China also aided the nuclear programs of Iran and Algeria as well as Iran's chemical and biological weapons program.

The level of China's arms sales has fallen in recent years, and China has shown restraint in its transfers to rogue states such as Iran and Iraq. In addition Beijing has increased its adherence to international agreements regulating the sale and spread of dangerous arms, although it is still not committed to the spirit of many of these agreements.

CHINA'S PRIMARY CUSTOMERS

Six countries—Pakistan, Iran, Iraq, North Korea, Myanmar, and Thailand—have been China's primary arms transfer recipients since the 1980s. Of these, Pakistan has been the most important. In addition to selling Islamabad large amounts of conventional weapons, in the 1980s China provided Pakistan with a proven nuclear weapon design and enough enriched uranium for two devices, and has since provided additional assistance to Pakistan's nuclear program. China also sold Pakistan components of M-11 short-range ballistic missiles and has provided assistance to Pakistan's indigenous ballistic missile program. China's interest in Pakistan is largely strategic. Both countries are strategic rivals of India, and during the Cold War Pakistan was an effective counter to Soviet influence in South and Southwest Asia. Today, relations with China are increasingly important to Pakistan, as ties to the West have diminished in the aftermath of the Cold War.

China has sold Iran large numbers of conventional weapons, supplied it with equipment and materials to produce chemical and biological weapons, and provided technical assistance to Iran's nuclear and ballistic missile programs. China's motivations for its arms sales to Iran have been strategic as well as commercial. In the 1980s, Beijing considered Iran a bulwark against Soviet expansionism. Today, China, which is increasingly dependent on imported oil, seeks close ties because Iran is a major oil exporter. Iran, for its part, has sought Chinese arms and technology primarily because they are available and cheap.

Iraq was a major recipient of Chinese arms in the 1980s, although China has adhered to the UN arms embargo against Iraq since Iraq's invasion of Kuwait in 1990. If UN sanctions are lifted, military coop-eration with Iraq will likely resume. As with Iran, China seeks not only commercial benefits but also to strengthen ties to important oil producers such as Iraq. Baghdad, for its part, will almost certainly try to rebuild its military, and the cheap price and ready availability of Chinese arms will make them attractive.

North Korea has received Chinese arms for many years, but transfers have diminished recently. During the Cold War, China sought to re-duce North Korea's dependence on the Soviet Union by providing conventional weapons; however, no new arms deals have apparently been signed since the late 1980s. With the collapse of the Soviet Union, an economic crisis in North Korea, and China's desire to avoid instability on the Korean peninsula, Beijing now maintains its influence in Pyongyang through other means. Arms sales are un-likely to resume until Pyongyang acquires the ability to pay with hard currency.

Myanmar has gone from purchasing no Chinese arms prior to 1989 to becoming one of China's most important customers for conven-tional weapons in the 1990s. As with Pakistan, Beijing seeks to use arms sales to Myanmar to complicate India's security planning. China also seeks to acquire access to Myanmar facilities in the Indian Ocean, protect China's commercial interests in Myanmar, and bol-ster a fellow authoritarian state in a democratizing world. Rangoon, which shares Beijing's concerns about New Delhi, has few alternative suppliers and appreciates Beijing's assistance with developing Myanmar's infrastructure.

Thailand was a major recipient of Chinese conventional weapons in the late 1980s and early 1990s, but the arms relationship appears to have ended. Thailand received weapons as gifts or at nominal prices. Beijing's motivations in making these transfers included countering Soviet and Vietnamese influence in Southeast Asia and extending Beijing's own influence in the region. Thailand accepted Chinese weapons to deter Vietnam, because Bangkok was not certain that the United States would continue to supply arms, and because of their low cost. Further significant arms transfers from China to Thailand are unlikely, however, because of Thai dissatisfaction with the quality of Chinese weapons, Vietnam's withdrawal from Cambodia, the renewed availability of U.S. arms, and Thailand's current economic difficulties.

MOTIVATIONS

Countries seek Chinese weapons because they are available, cheap, and easy to use and maintain. China is one of the few countries willing to sell arms to "pariah" states such as Iran, North Korea, and Myanmar. Beijing also has been willing to pass on technology related to nuclear and chemical weapons as well as to ballistic missiles. Demand for Chinese conventional weapons has fallen significantly since the 1980s, however, as a result of the ending of the Iran-Iraq war, a decline in interest in cheap Chinese weapons after Operation Desert Storm, and the availability of more advanced Russian designs.

On the supply side, China's arms sales can be explained by a combination of strategic and commercial motivations. Strategic concerns include a desire to strengthen foes of China's rivals and to expand China's political influence in regions such as the Middle East and Southeast Asia. China also seeks to maintain its defense industries in the face of diminished domestic procurement, generate foreign exchange earnings for the country as a whole and for the defense industries in particular, subsidize research and development programs by including foreign recipients in the customer base, and stimulate technological progress by competing in foreign markets.

In general, however, strategic factors outweigh commercial ones. Arms sales represented a significant portion (roughly 7 percent) of China's export earnings in the 1980s, but today they are only a small fraction of China's total sales abroad. Indeed, many of China's recent transfers were subsidized, and Beijing has refrained from sales to possible foes, indicating that strategic concerns guide most sales.

SOURCES OF RESTRAINT

China's attitudes toward the dangers posed by arms sales and proliferation have gradually evolved into a more nuanced understanding of the problem and the costs involved in remaining outside the international nonproliferation community. Prior to the 1980s, China opposed limitations on arms transfers. Since 1992, however, China has joined a number of nonproliferation regimes and has generally complied with the letter, if not the spirit, of these agreements. Increasingly, Chinese officials appear aware of some of the dangers of proliferation.

Beijing continues to contribute to the NBC and missile programs of other states, but it does so through loopholes in existing regimes. China provided nuclear assistance to Iran and Algeria, but this assistance was consistent with the Non-Proliferation Treaty (NPT). In 1995, however, China transferred ring magnets to Pakistan, in probable violation of the NPT (although these magnets are not explicitly mentioned on the International Atomic Energy Agency [IAEA] Trigger List). Similarly, China has provided Iran with equipment and materials that could be used in the manufacturing of chemical and biological weapons, although this equipment is not banned by the Chemical Weapons Convention or Biological Warfare Convention. In 1992, China pledged to abide by the Missile Technology Control Regime (MTCR), but violated its spirit later that year when it transferred M-11 ballistic missile components to Pakistan. China has not transferred complete systems since reaffirming its commitment to the MTCR in 1994, but has continued to provide technical assistance to the ballistic missile programs of Iran and Pakistan.

The United States has a modest ability to influence China's arms transfers. Beijing wishes to be seen as a responsible member of the international community, and the United States has used this desire to prevent certain transfers—particularly those to Iran and Iraq. Control over important technology provides the United States with another source of influence over China's arms transfers. Nonetheless, Beijing is sensitive to the appearance of a double standard with regard to arms transfers and is resistant to the idea that it should curtail its arms sales to countries objectionable to the United States.

Greater allied support would facilitate U.S. ability to influence Beijing.

The argument that China's arms transfers are not under Beijing's control is fallacious. All important arms sales must have the approval of the top leadership. The export control system for dual-use equipment and technology is much weaker, by contrast, and it is possible that dual-use goods that violate China's various nonproliferation commitments could be transferred without the knowledge of China's leadership. However, Beijing has been strengthening its export control regulations in recent years.

POLICY IMPLICATIONS

Regardless of U.S. efforts to limit China's arms sales, some transfers will inevitably occur. Most of China's conventional weapons are unsophisticated and do not present a significant threat to the United States if transferred. Of most concern are China's transfers of technology related to nuclear weapons, chemical weapons, and missiles. Given the limitations on the U.S. ability to stop these transfers, the U.S. military in general, and the U.S. Air Force in particular, must prepare for the possibility of future conflict with regional adversaries, such as Iran, who are armed with longer-range ballistic missiles and perhaps even nuclear or chemical weapons.

ACKNOWLEDGMENTS

The authors gratefully acknowledge the help of many RAND colleagues, who gave generously of their time and expertise. Zalmay Khalilzad provided overall direction for this effort, and Alan Vick and C. R. Neu offered valuable comments and suggestions, strengthening the analysis. Bates Gill provided a thorough and valuable review.

Individuals in the Air Force Regional Plans and Issues office played an important role in both this project's inception and its development. Thanks go to Major Milt Johnson and Major Steve Cunico for their assistance.

Any mistakes remain the authors' alone.

Chapter One

INTRODUCTION

Since the 1980s, China has been a major supplier of weapons and technology of concern to the United States and other countries. Not only has China sold large quantities of conventional arms to rogue states such as Iran, it has also transferred technology that can be used in the production of missiles (along with complete missile systems) and nuclear, biological, and chemical (NBC) weapons to several nations, including potential U.S. adversaries. In June 1997, the Director of Central Intelligence testified to Congress that "China was the most significant supplier of NBC-related goods and technologies to foreign countries."[1] Although many countries sell a greater volume of arms than does China, Beijing has not exercised the same restraint that Western countries have. France, Britain, and the United States all are major suppliers, but in general they have refrained from transferring NBC-related technologies and are careful in the arms they sell to states that support terrorism or threaten their neighbors.

China's arms transfer behavior has become less dangerous in recent years because of both external and internal factors. The end of the Iran-Iraq war in 1988 resulted in a sharply diminished demand for Chinese conventional arms from those two countries, which had been China's largest customers. Operation Desert Storm dramatically demonstrated the inferiority of the low-tech systems China produces, further decreasing demand. The collapse of China's rival,

---

[1] As quoted in Shirley A. Kan, *China's Compliance with International Arms Control Agreements*, CRS Report to Congress, Washington DC: Congressional Research Service, updated January 16, 1998, p. 1.

the Soviet Union, has made more-advanced Russian equipment available at cut-rate prices in what some analysts have described as "the fire sale at the end of history." Developments at home have also led sales to decrease. In the early 1990s, perhaps to reduce China's isolation resulting from the 1989 Tiananmen Square killings, the Chinese leadership began increasing its participation in a number of international regimes, including those directed at controlling the proliferation of nuclear, biological, and chemical weapons. The enduring effect of these internal and external changes is not clear, however, and concerns about continued proliferation and transfers to rogue states are warranted.

This study examines China's recent arms transfer behavior, with particular emphasis on changes that have been occurring since the late 1980s. After summarizing the history of China's arms sales since the late 1970s, the report addresses the issue of which types of arms transfer are of greatest concern for the United States. China's major arms relationships since the late 1970s are then examined in detail. The study next examines China's strategic and commercial motivations for arms transfers and factors that may cause Beijing to exercise restraint in its arms sales. The issue of whether Beijing actually controls China's arms sales is assessed, as is the ability of the United States to affect Beijing's behavior. The report concludes by noting the implications of China's arms sales for U.S. interests.

Chapter Two

BACKGROUND

Prior to the late 1970s, China supplied arms mostly to revolutionary governments or movements, particularly in the developing world, including Angola, Tanzania, Congo, Sierra Leone, Sudan, and Zaire. In keeping with the pre–Deng Xiaoping emphasis on revolutionary solidarity, China's motivations were more ideological than financial.[1] Even though China at this time had a highly ideological foreign policy, many of Beijing's most important transfers, including those to North Vietnam, Pakistan, and North Korea, were made for security reasons.[2] After the Sino-Soviet split in the early 1960s, China provided arms and military aid to Albania and North Korea to keep them independent of Moscow. Beijing also moved closer to Pakistan, a major regional Soviet adversary, even though its ideology had little to do with Maoism.[3]

In the late 1970s, however, there was a fundamental shift in China's approach to arms transfers. Beijing began selling arms to new customers, such as Bangladesh, Myanmar, Egypt, Iran, Iraq, and Thailand, while sales to African countries dropped off. Most of China's sales went to the Middle East, particularly to Iraq and Iran

---

[1]For an overview of China's arms transfers prior to the 1980s, see R. Bates Gill, *Chinese Arms Transfers: Purposes, Patterns, and Prospects in the New World Order,* Praeger, Westport, CT, 1992.

[2]Richard A. Bitzinger, "Arms to Go: Chinese Arms Sales to the Third World," *International Security,* Vol. 17, No. 2, Fall 1992, p. 85; Karl W. Eikenberry, *Explaining and Influencing Chinese Arms Transfers,* McNair Paper 36, Institute for National Strategic Studies, National Defense University, Washington DC, 1995, pp. 5–15.

[3]Bitzinger, "Arms to Go," pp. 85–86.

during the bitter war these two countries fought from 1980 to 1988.[4] By the mid-1980s, China was the world's fourth largest arms supplier (after the Soviet Union, United States, and France).[5]

Most of the weapons China has transferred have been relatively low-tech, consisting primarily of Chinese copies of 1950s and 1960s Soviet systems (although the Chinese products have been said to be of higher quality than the original Soviet equipment).[6] The Type-59 tank, for example, is the Chinese version of the Soviet T-54, while the F-6 and F-7 fighter jets are Chinese versions of the MiG-19 and MiG-21. Even the notorious HY-2 "Silkworm" antishipping missile is simply an improved version of the Soviet 1950s-era P-15 "Styx" system. These weapons are generally less capable than systems currently sold by Western countries or Russia and have often been used to equip second-line units or to pad out the military inventories of the recipient nations. The systems transferred have not represented a serious threat to stability or security.[7] A list of China's transfers in the 1980s and 1990s is presented in the appendix.

Beginning in the late 1980s, however, China began to make arms transfers that were much more worrisome. In 1987, China sold nuclear-capable intermediate-range ballistic missiles to Saudi Arabia.[8] In the same year, Iran used Chinese-made Silkworm missiles to disrupt shipping in the Persian Gulf. China's refusal to curtail or even admit to these sales prompted the United States to delay liberalization of technology sales to China, the first instance of a U.S. sanction on China since the normalization of relations in 1978.[9] At about the

---

[4]Bitzinger, "Arms to Go," p. 87. Iran and Iraq accounted for 57 percent of Chinese arms sales during the 1980s.

[5]Stockholm International Peace Research Institute, *SIPRI Yearbook 1992: Armaments, Disarmament, and International Security*, Oxford University Press, Oxford, New York, 1992, p. 272.

[6]"Birth of an Arms Salesman," *The Economist*, November 17, 1984, p. 40.

[7]Francois Godemont, "China's Arms Sales," in Gerald Segal and Richard H. Yang (eds.), *Chinese Economic Reform: The Impact on Security*, Routledge, London and New York, 1996, p. 98.

[8]Shirley A. Kan, *Chinese Proliferation of Weapons of Mass Destruction: Background and Analysis*, CRS Report for Congress, Congressional Research Service, Washington DC, September 13, 1996, p. 14.

[9]Nayan Chanda, "Technology Cocooned," *Far Eastern Economic Review*, November 5, 1987, p. 34.

same time, China reportedly came to an agreement with Syria to sell it M-9 short-range ballistic missiles (SRBMs). This sale was apparently never consummated as a result of U.S. and Israeli pressure, but China did transfer components of the M-11 SRBM to Pakistan in 1991–1992 and has provided technical assistance to the ballistic missile programs in both Pakistan and Iran. China also subsequently transferred more antishipping cruise missiles, in this case the more advanced C-801 and C-802, despite U.S. protests.

Even more alarming was China's assistance to the nuclear programs of several countries. China reportedly provided significant assistance to Pakistan's clandestine nuclear weapons program in the 1980s, including supplying it with a nuclear weapon design and fissile material. Beijing continued to provide further nuclear assistance in the 1990s, although perhaps no longer directly to Pakistan's nuclear weapons program.[10] China also assisted the nuclear programs of Iran and Algeria. Although this assistance was ostensibly for research and therefore was consistent with the terms of the Non-Proliferation Treaty (NPT) (which China did not sign until 1992), both Iran and Algeria had large undeveloped energy reserves and appeared to lack a legitimate need for nuclear power, leading to suspicions that their true purpose was to develop the expertise needed for producing nuclear weapons. In addition to its nuclear assistance to Iran, China has been accused of contributing to Iran's chemical weapons program.

The nature of the recipients of many Chinese arms transfers is cause for concern. Customers have included Iran, Iraq, North Korea, and Myanmar, which are among the world's leading pariah states, and Pakistan, which has refused to join the nuclear nonproliferation regime and recently tested several nuclear weapons. China's arms transfers and their recipients have caused concern throughout the world and highlighted the question of whether China wishes to be a responsible member of the international community.

In sum, China's arms transfer record is troubling. China has transferred equipment and technology related to missiles and nuclear and

---

[10]Kan, *Chinese Proliferation of Weapons of Mass Destruction*, pp. 27–31.

chemical weapons, and its customers have included states that other nations are unwilling to sell to. Understanding the motivations for these sales and ways to limit them is an important task.

Chapter Three

EXPLAINING CHINA'S ARMS TRANSFERS

A range of factors determines the scope and scale of China's arms sales. As with any other commodity, China's arms sales are the result of a combination of supply-side and demand-side factors. The weapons' quality and price and purchasers' desire to improve political ties to Beijing are two primary drivers of demand. China's customers also often are seeking to diversify supply sources or, conversely, lack alternative supply sources. China's supply-side considerations include the desire to improve political ties with the recipient country, efforts to use the recipient state to balance against a strategic rival, and purely commercial considerations. No single determinant dominates either the demand or supply for weapons; which determinants are most prominent vary by the country involved. This chapter first examines China's major arms transfer relationships and then assesses the major determinants.

CHINA'S PRINCIPAL ARMS TRANSFER RELATIONSHIPS

Although China has transferred arms and weapons technology to nearly two dozen countries since 1980, arms transfers to six countries—Iran, Iraq, Pakistan, North Korea, Myanmar, and Thailand—are of particular significance. Sales to these countries are worthy of close examination because of the volume of weapons transferred, the nature of the recipient regime, and/or because the transfers involve missile systems or NBC weapons.[1]

---

[1]The information in this chapter is not a definitive documentation of the scope and scale of China's arms transfers or of the particulars of various sales. Rather, this chap-

Iran

China has had extensive military relations with Iran. Beijing has sold thousands of tanks, artillery pieces, and armored personnel carriers to Iran, more than 100 combat aircraft, and dozens of small warships. Beijing has also sold Iran an array of missile systems and technology, including air-to-air missiles, surface-to-air missiles, and antishipping cruise missiles. Most worrisome have been China's transfer of ballistic missile technology and its assistance with Iran's NBC programs. Cooperation in these areas continued at a robust pace until at least 1997. In September 1996, China and Iran signed a deal whereby China would provide combat aircraft, warships, a variety of armored vehicles, missile and electronic equipment, and military training to Iran.[2] In October 1997, however, China agreed to suspend or curtail transfers of NBC-related items as well as antishipping missile systems and technology.

China has provided a range of assistance to Iran's NBC programs:

- China has sent entire factories to Iran for producing chemicals that, although they have legitimate purposes, can also be used to make poison gas, and tons of industrial chemicals that could be used in making nerve agents.[3]

- State-owned firms in China provided supplies to Iran's chemical weapons program, including such dual-use items as chemical precursors, production equipment, and production technology.[4] Non-state-owned firms may also have sold chemical-related

---

ter provides a detailed overview of China's most important arms transfer relationships for the purpose of analyzing the driving forces.

[2]Bates Gill, *Silkworms and Summitry: Chinese Arms Exports to Iran and U.S.-China Relations,* The Asia and Pacific Rim Institute of the American Jewish Committee, New York, 1997, p. 25.

[3]Gary Milhollin, testimony before the Senate Intelligence Committee, September 18, 1997.

[4]Kan, *China's Compliance with International Arms Control Agreements,* p. 1; U.S. Congress, Senate Governmental Affairs Subcommittee on International Security, Proliferation, and Federal Services, *China: Proliferation Case Studies,* Hearing on April 10, 1997, 105th Congress, Session 1, 1997, p. 8.

equipment, decontamination agents, and precursors to Iranian military organizations in 1996 and 1997.[5]

- U.S. intelligence reports leaked to the press indicate China may have sold Iran dual-use equipment and vaccines for biological weapons.[6]

- China has transferred nuclear technology and know-how to Iran's civilian nuclear programs, thus improving Tehran's ability to make nuclear weapons. China's assistance, all of which is technically acceptable under the International Atomic Energy Agency's (IAEA's) guidelines, has included help with uranium mining and enrichment, research reactors, production facility blueprints, and technical training. Beijing trained perhaps 15 Iranian nuclear engineers between 1988 and 1992.[7] Chinese nuclear experts traveled to Iran in 1996 to help build a new uranium conversion plant.[8]

- China has provided a range of assistance to Iran's missile programs, and may have helped Iran build its large missile factory at Isfahan. China also helped build another plant and a test range near Tehran and is providing assistance guidance technologies and precision machine tools for Iran's indigenous programs.[9] China helped Iran's Zelzal-3 (with 1000-km range) program with solid-fuel technology, gyroscopes, and guidance.[10] In addition,

---

[5]Kan, *China's Compliance with International Arms Control Agreements*, pp. 10–11; Robert Karniol, "China Supplied Iran with Decontamination Agent," *Jane's Defense Weekly*, April 30, 1997, p. 17.

[6]U.S. Congress, Subcommittee on International Security, Proliferation, and Federal Services, *The Proliferation Primer*, Washington DC, 1998, p. 8.

[7]Gill, *Silkworms and Summitry*, pp. 12–13; Frank J. Gaffney, "China Arms the Rogues," *Middle East Quarterly*, September 1997, p. 34.

[8]China is also building a small nuclear reactor with Iran and a factory to encase fuel rods for reactors—projects U.S. officials claim are not important for proliferation—and promises no new nuclear cooperation with Iran. Kan, *China's Compliance with International Arms Control Agreements*, p. 9.

[9]Gill, *Silkworms and Summitry*, p. 11.

[10]Gill, *Silkworms and Summitry*, p. 12.

> Chinese experts are reportedly working at Iranian missile pro-
> duction complexes.[11]

As the above overview makes clear, China's transfers to Iran are not
limited to complete systems. China has also transferred scientific
expertise, technology, and dual-use items to Iran, as well as motors
and test equipment for a short-range Iranian missile, the NP-110.[12]
As a result of Beijing's assistance, Iran has developed variants of
Chinese systems and now can produce several indigenously.[13]
Gauging the true extent of such transfers is difficult. Beijing has
regularly denied that it has transferred weapons systems, particularly
cruise missiles and NBC technology, and it is difficult to confirm the
transfer of knowledge and production assistance.

China's cooperation with Iran appears to have diminished in recent
years, partly because of U.S. pressure. In October 1997, China agreed
not to provide new assistance to Iran's nuclear programs, and in
January 1998, Secretary of Defense Cohen received an assurance
from Chinese President Jiang Zemin that China would not transfer
additional antiship cruise missiles or technology to Iran or help it
with indigenous production.[14]

The commercial benefits of China's sales to Iran have been considerable, particularly during the Iran-Iraq war. China sold billions of
dollars' worth of arms to Iran during the 1980s, and these sales provided Beijing with much-needed foreign currency. Since the end of
the Iran-Iraq war, the volume of Beijing's sales to Iran has fallen
considerably while China's overall trade has skyrocketed, but export
earnings are still an important source of income for some of China's
cash-strapped defense industries.

---

[11]Shirley A. Kan, *Chinese Proliferation of Weapons of Mass Destruction: Current Policy
Issues*, CRS Issue Brief, Congressional Research Service, Washington DC, March 23,
1998, p. 12.

[12]Bill Gertz, "Nuclear Sales to China Too Chancy, Foes Insist," *The Washington Times*,
October 28, 1997, p. 1.

[13]Gill, *Silkworms and Summitry*, p. 22.

[14]Kan, *Chinese Proliferation of Weapons of Mass Destruction: Current Policy Issues*,
p. 6.

China sells arms to Iran for foreign policy as well as commercial reasons. Until recently, China had a strong strategic and political interest in maintaining close ties with Iran. China's leaders considered Iran a bulwark against Soviet expansion in the region. Even today, Beijing appreciates Tehran's attempts to avoid aligning closely with Russia or the United States.[15] And because most regional oil-producing states are close allies of the United States, Beijing seeks to ensure at least a modicum of influence in the region by maintaining good relations with Tehran.

Beijing also recognizes that preventing Iran from improving its military is a U.S. priority, and it may exploit U.S. sensitivity on this issue to attempt to influence U.S. policies in other areas. For example, after the United States announced it was selling F-16s to Taiwan, China revived a proposed transfer of M-11 missiles to Iran, which had earlier been canceled because of U.S. pressure.[16] Ties to Iran thus provide Beijing with additional leverage in negotiations with the United States.

Chinese interest in maintaining the flow of oil has led Beijing to cultivate relations with Tehran, although this could change in the coming years. China's dependence on imported oil has grown steadily since 1994, and it is likely to continue to do so in the future. Thus, China seeks allies in key oil-producing regions, such as the Persian Gulf. In a crisis these countries are not likely to sell China oil on preferential terms, but Chinese analysts believe that maintaining good relations with leading oil-exporting nations such as Iran is important to China's future energy security.[17] The United States, however, has attempted to convince Beijing that Iranian-backed instability threatens the free flow of oil from the Gulf, which could drive up the price of oil and jeopardize China's economic growth. U.S. officials claimed that China's promises at the October 1997 summit to

---

[15]Gill, *Silkworms and Summitry*, p. 7.

[16]Gill, *Silkworms and Summitry*, p. 21.

[17]Interviews conducted with the Institute of West Asian and African Studies, Chinese Academy of Social Sciences, June 1998.

cut nuclear cooperation with Iran occurred in large part because China recognized this danger.[18]

Iran, for its part, sees China as an important political partner and as a source of lethal weapons systems. China, with its UN seat and desire to reduce U.S. hegemony, was one of the few major powers willing to maintain strong and cordial relations with Tehran during the more radical days of the revolutionary regime. Perhaps more important, Tehran greatly appreciated Beijing's willingness to support Iran's missile and NBC programs. Moreover, because Iran, like China, seeks to avoid import dependence, Beijing is often a preferred partner—willing to transfer knowledge and expertise as well as critical subsystems. This has enabled Iran to produce its own variants of Chinese cruise and ballistic missile systems.

China, however, is not Iran's preferred partner for most conventional systems. After the Persian Gulf war, Tehran bought advanced submarines, fighter aircraft, tanks, and surface-to-air missiles from Russia: the Chinese systems, while cheaper, were clearly inferior, and the U.S. success in Desert Storm had shown the importance of advanced weaponry. Only after 1995, when Russia pledged that it would not make further arms contracts with Iran, did Tehran resume looking to China for conventional arms.

In recent years, China's relations with Iran appear to have cooled and the transfer of arms has fallen in turn. The ending of the Iran-Iraq war and the low price of oil mean that Iran no longer has the need or the ability to buy large quantities of Chinese arms. U.S. sanctions and economic mismanagement have caused grave economic problems for the Islamic republic, forcing it to reduce its defense budget. In addition, Iranian military officials probably have little faith in the quality of Chinese weapons: during the Iran-Iraq war, they sought to avoid using Chinese systems whenever possible during major battles. At the same time, the collapse of the Soviet Union means that more sophisticated Russian weapons are now available at equally low prices.

---

[18]"A New China Embracing Nuclear Nonproliferation," *International Herald Tribune*, December 11, 1997, p. 1.

For its part, China no longer sees Iran as a vital bulwark against Soviet expansion. Indeed, China often cooperates with Russia against the West. U.S. pressure and China's desire to be seen as a responsible power make Iran a potentially costly friend for Beijing. U.S. pressure played a major role in Beijing's October 1997 decision to curtail military cooperation with Iran.

Iraq

From 1983 to 1989, Baghdad received over $5 billion worth of arms from China,[19] including an array of conventional systems ranging from tanks to fighter aircraft. Despite their limited sophistication, Chinese weapons proved relatively easy for the poorly trained Iraqi forces to use.

Beijing has adhered to the 1990 UN sanctions on Iraq, but arms sales may well resume if sanctions are lifted. If sanctions end, China will almost certainly seek to increase cooperation with Baghdad regarding oil and may renew military cooperation in return.[20] A top priority under Saddam or any likely successor government will be to rebuild Iraq's military. Moreover, Iraq may not trust the few Western states, such as France, that are likely to sell it arms. Like Iran, Iraq also seeks to produce its own weapons systems and thus will welcome Chinese transfers of knowledge and production assistance. As a result, China—along with Russia—could be faced with a wealthy customer eager to make major purchases. Such sales would pose a threat to U.S. interests, as Iraq remains unremittingly hostile to U.S. allies in the region and is pursuing NBC programs.

Relations with Iraq follow the same logic as relations with Iran. Iraq's immense oil reserves—by some estimates 10 percent of the world's total known assets—increase its attractiveness to Beijing. Just as China has sought good relations with Iran because of its oil assets, so too will it seek close, or at least cordial, relations with Baghdad, if possible. Iraq's hostility toward the West also has some

---

[19]Anthony H. Cordesman and Ahmed S. Hashim, *Iraq: Sanctions and Beyond,* Westview, Boulder, CO, 1997, p. 227.

[20]Interviews conducted at the Institute of Eurasian Studies, Shanghai Academy of Social Sciences, May 1998.

strategic attraction for Beijing, offering another potential ally in this U.S.-dominated region.

Pakistan

Pakistan has been China's most significant recipient of weapons and military technology. Islamabad is at least a nominal ally of Washington, and thus conventional arms sold to Pakistan should pose little threat. However, the repeated transfer of NBC technology and associated delivery systems make this relationship of particular concern to the United States. China has sold or even given Pakistan Type-59 tanks, Type-531 armored personnel carriers, missile boats, F-7P jet fighters, and M-11 missiles among other systems.[21] China has also provided Pakistan with facilities to produce an array of conventional systems including jet trainers, the Type-69 tank, the HJ-8 antitank missile, and the HN-5A portable surface-to-air missile.[22]

In addition, China has been willing to incur the wrath of the United States to help Pakistan's missile and NBC programs even though the financial reward is limited:

- Beijing played a major role in Pakistan's nuclear program. In the 1980s, China reportedly provided Pakistan with a proven nuclear weapon design and enough highly enriched uranium for two weapons.[23] A high level of cooperation has continued in the 1990s. In 1994 or 1995, a Chinese government-owned subsidiary transferred 5000 ring magnets, which are used in centrifuges to enrich uranium, to unsafeguarded facilities in Pakistan, a shipment worth $70,000 that violated China's NPT obligations in the opinion of Administration officials and outside experts.[24] At

---

[21]Eric Hyer, "China's Arms Merchants: Profits in Command," *The China Quarterly,* No. 132, December 1992, p. 1105.

[22]Eikenberry, *Explaining and Influencing Chinese Arms Transfers*, pp. 5–15.

[23]Gary Milhollin, testimony before the Senate Intelligence Committee, September 18, 1997.

[24]See testimony of Gary Milhollin, U.S. Congress, Senate Governmental Affairs Subcommittee on International Security, Proliferation, and Federal Services, *China: Proliferation Case Studies*, Hearing on April 19, 1997, 105th Congress, Session 1, 1997, p. 31; and the testimony of Under Secretary of State Lynn Davis, U.S. Congress, House

about the same time, China also sold Pakistan dual-use technology—diagnostic equipment and an industrial furnace—that can be used for nuclear weapons.[25]

- China has also played an active role in Pakistan's missile program. For example, in November 1992 China transferred M-11 short-range ballistic missile components to Pakistan, and in August 1993 China shipped additional equipment related to the M-11 missiles. Intelligence reports leaked to the media indicate China sent missile parts to Pakistan in 1995.[26] Pakistan is developing the Ghauri, a 1500-km-range ballistic missile, probably with Chinese assistance. China may also have provided blueprints and equipment to Pakistan for manufacturing M-11 missile components and perhaps whole missiles.[27]

Pakistan was a particularly important ally for China during the Cold War, representing a bulwark against Soviet expansion in Afghanistan and a staunch foe of Moscow in general. The two countries worked together with the United States to arm the Afghan *mujahedin* and to prevent Soviet expansion. Now that the Soviet threat is gone, the greatest strategic benefit to both countries is to offset Indian military power. Both China and Pakistan have fought wars with India, and India has supported Tibetan dissidents against Beijing. The May 1998 Indian nuclear tests were ostensibly directed against China, increasing Beijing's shared strategic concerns with Islamabad. China's arms sales and military cooperation in general with Pakistan increase Beijing's military leverage over New Delhi. By strengthening Pakistan's military capabilities, China forces India to devote more resources to its border with Pakistan and less to its border with China.[28]

International Relations Committee Hearing, *Review of the Clinton Administration Nonproliferation Policy*, 104th Congress, 2nd Session, June 19, 1995, p. 15.

[25]Bill Gertz, "Beijing Flouts Nuke-Sales Ban," *Washington Times*, October 9, 1996, p. A1.

[26]Kan, *China's Compliance with International Arms Control Agreements*, p. 3.

[27]R. Jeffrey Smith, "China Linked to Pakistani Missile Plant: Secret Project Could Renew Sanctions Issue," *Washington Post*, August 25, 1996, p. A1.

[28]Robert E. Mullins, "The Dynamics of Chinese Missile Proliferation," *The Pacific Review*, Vol. 8, No. 1, 1995, p. 142.

Ties to Pakistan enhance Beijing's strategic and political reach. Karachi is a regular refueling point for Chinese aircraft flying to Europe, Africa, and the Middle East, and Pakistan acts as a go-between for China and various Islamic countries, helping facilitate China's relations with Iran, Saudi Arabia, and other Muslim nations.[29]

On the other hand, Pakistan also has close ties with the Muslim movements in Afghanistan, a potential pitfall in China's relationship with Pakistan. Pakistan has funded, armed, and organized the Taliban, the dominant faction in Afghanistan. The Taliban, in turn, have probably aided Muslim radicals operating in China itself, including Uighur separatists and other violent groups in Xinjiang. Surprisingly, these ties have so far not affected Pakistan's close ties to China. Continued Afghan aid to activists in China, however, could affect Beijing's relations with Islamabad.

Islamabad, for its part, increasingly needs Beijing as a strategic ally. Western nations, particularly the United States, have distanced themselves from Pakistan because of its nuclear program. Other countries, such as Russia, may be hesitant to jeopardize lucrative ties to India in order to improve relations with Pakistan. Thus, China is the only major arms supplier willing to work with Islamabad consistently.

Arms sales to Pakistan are thus likely to remain steady in the coming years. Pakistan is one of Beijing's few close allies, and the two countries' mutual fear of India will keep military relations on track. Pakistan's economy, however, has stagnated in recent years, which will make it difficult for Islamabad to increase purchases of Chinese equipment. Anger over Pakistan's support for the Taliban could also lead Beijing to restrict its arms sales to Pakistan.

North Korea

North Korea has been one of China's steady arms customers over the years and transfers continued into the early 1990s. Although the volume has not been enormous, it is significant because North Korea

---

[29]*Ibid.*

continues to threaten the forces of the United States and its South Korean ally. Transfers since 1980 have included Romeo-class submarines, F-6 fighters, HY-2 ("Silkworm") antishipping missiles, HN-5A man-portable surface-to-air missiles, and multiple launch rocket systems.[30]

Beijing's motivations for arms transfers to North Korea primarily have been strategic. China and North Korea became allies during the Korean War in 1950, and in the 1950s Chinese officials described the relationship between the two socialist countries as being "as close as lips and teeth." After the Sino-Soviet break in 1960, Beijing had an even stronger interest in maintaining good relations with Pyongyang—a North Korea that tilted toward the Soviet Union would have presented a serious security problem for China. With the launching of China's economic reform program in the late 1970s, China's leaders stressed the importance of a peaceful international environment for China's economic development. China's leadership thus had a renewed interest in maintaining its influence in Pyongyang to dissuade North Korean leaders from provoking a conflict with South Korea, even as concerns about Soviet encirclement faded in the late 1980s.

Arms sales have been one way of ensuring this influence.[31] Although no new arms deals between China and North Korea have apparently been concluded since the late 1980s, this may be a result of Pyongyang's inability to pay for additional armaments rather than Beijing's unwillingness to continue to supply arms to North Korea.[32] As two of the few remaining socialist countries, relations between China and North Korea have remained cordial in the 1990s, despite Beijing's recognition of Seoul in 1992. China now maintains its goodwill in Pyongyang through the shipments of food and energy supplies it provides. Given Beijing's desire to avoid hostilities (or economic collapse) on the Korean peninsula, these supplies are probably viewed as a more prudent way to cultivate relations with

---

[30]Stockholm International Peace Research Institute, *SIPRI Yearbook*, 1983–1997 editions, Oxford University Press, Oxford, New York, 1983–1997.

[31]It is unclear whether these were provided at market or "friendship" prices.

[32]Stockholm International Peace Research Institute, *SIPRI Yearbook*, 1983–1997 editions; Tai Ming Cheung, "Proliferation Is Good, and There's Money in It Too," *Far Eastern Economic Review*, June 2, 1988, p. 26.

Pyongyang than through free or subsidized arms shipments.[33] Thus, it seems unlikely that China will conduct significant further weapons sales with North Korea, at least until North Korea acquires the ability to pay for them in hard currency at market prices.

North Korea has purchased Chinese weapons primarily because China and the Soviet bloc have been the two sources available to it. Pyongyang presumably felt solidarity with its fellow socialist countries, but limiting its purchases to China and the Soviet bloc also was out of necessity. Most Western nations would have refused to sell weapons to the violent and hostile North Korean regime. Although the majority of North Korea's arms in the 1980s and 1990s were from Russia, probably because Soviet arms sales were made at subsidized rates, the North Korean leadership has attempted to play Beijing and Moscow off against each other to maximize its leverage with both. This explains why Pyongyang purchased Chinese weapons as well.[34]

The collapse of the Soviet Union has meant the end of Soviet subsidies to North Korea, reducing China's imperative for good relations with Pyongyang. Pyongyang has signed virtually no new weapons agreements with any country since the late 1980s, although in the early 1990s it continued to receive deliveries of Russian and Chinese systems for which it had previously contracted.[35] Chinese arms sales to North Korea totaled over $1 billion in the 1980s but amounted to less than $50 million in the first half of the 1990s.[36] Although Pyongyang will probably prefer to purchase Chinese and Russian systems in the future because of their compatibility with its existing inventory, its desperate economic straits and lack of foreign exchange leave it unable to pay for these weapons.

---

[33]Interviews at Institute of Asia-Pacific Studies, Shanghai Academy of Social Sciences, May 1998; at China Institute for International Studies, June 1998; and at China Institute for Contemporary International Relations, June 1998.

[34]Gill, *Chinese Arms Transfers*, p. 192.

[35]Stockholm International Peace Research Institute, *SIPRI Yearbook*, 1983–1997 editions.

[36]Bates Gill, "Chinese Military Modernization and Arms Proliferation in the Asia-Pacific," in Jonathan D. Pollack and Richard H. Yang (eds.), *In China's Shadow: Regional Perspectives on Chinese Foreign Policy and Military Development*, RAND, 1998, p. 25.

Myanmar

Myanmar has only recently become one of China's arms clients, with shipments of Type-62 and Type-63 light tanks beginning in 1989. Since that time, Myanmar has become an important customer for Chinese conventional weapons. Systems supplied to Myanmar include Type-69 main battle tanks, F-6 and F-7 fighter jets, A-5 attack aircraft, PL-2 air-to-air missiles, HN-5A portable surface-to-air missiles, Hainan-class patrol craft, multiple rocket launchers, Y-8 and Y-12 transport aircraft, and fire control radars.[37]

China has several interests in Myanmar. First, China's arms sales to Myanmar—like its sales to Pakistan—complicate the security planning of China's strategic rival, India.[38] The effort appears to be successful—Indian leaders and analysts have complained about Chinese encirclement.[39] In addition, China has apparently received access to Myanmar's Indian Ocean naval bases, including a radar installation on the Coco islands that is close to India's naval base in the adjoining Andaman Islands, in return for arms shipments and technical assistance to Myanmar's navy.[40] India and the Indian Ocean are said to be China's third greatest strategic concern after Taiwan and the South China Sea,[41] so China would appear to have a strong interest in continuing access to Myanmar's naval facilities.

Aside from its rivalry with India, Beijing has other reasons for wishing to maintain good relations with Yangon. First, China's commercial interests in Myanmar have been growing rapidly. Although China's

[37]Stockholm International Peace Research Institute, *SIPRI Yearbook,* 1983–1997 editions; Gill, "Chinese Military Modernization," p. 25.

[38]Interview at Institute of Asia-Pacific Studies, Shanghai Academy of Social Sciences, May 1998.

[39]"A militarized, China-supported Burma to the east is the last thing India needs at the moment" according to an Indian security official. Bertil Lintner, ". . . But Stay on Guard," *Far Eastern Economic Review,* July 16, 1998, p. 21.

[40]Karl W. Eikenberry, *Explaining and Influencing Chinese Arms Transfers,* p. 22; Bertil Lintner, "Arms for Eyes," *Far Eastern Economic Review,* December 16, 1993, p. 26; Bertil Lintner, "Burma Road," *Far Eastern Economic Review,* November 6, 1997, pp. 16–17; Lintner, ". . . But Stay on Guard," p. 21.

[41]Tai Ming Cheung, Hong Kong-based military analyst, quoted in Lintner, ". . . But Stay on Guard," p. 21.

trade with Myanmar has been less than $1 billion a year,[42] its greater significance is Myanmar's outlet for China's backward southwestern provinces. Also, mainland Chinese are heavily involved in commerce within Myanmar, and Beijing may wish to maintain good relations with Yangon to ensure that their interests are protected.[43] In addition, Beijing seeks influence over Yangon to limit drug smuggling from Myanmar into China. Finally, as a fellow authoritarian state in a democratizing world, Myanmar can provide political support to China in its efforts to delegitimatize criticism of human rights records as interference in states' internal political affairs. Given this combination of strategic, economic, and political interests, China is likely to remain eager to sell arms to Myanmar, quite possibly at subsidized rates, for the foreseeable future.

As with North Korea, the closed nature of Myanmar's political system means that information about Myanmar motivations in acquiring Chinese arms is scarce. Up until 1988, Yangon's purchases of foreign-made weapons had consisted primarily of training aircraft and transports.[44] After 1988, however, the Myanmar government suddenly began building up its armed forces. This may have been to placate the powerful armed forces or because of a perceived threat from India after Yangon's crushing of a pro-democracy uprising (which had Indian sympathy) in 1988. In any case, Myanmar began receiving major shipments of Chinese weapons beginning in 1989.[45]

Myanmar chose China as its arms supplier for both political reasons and out of necessity. After the Myanmar government's crackdown on pro-democracy demonstrators, most Western countries were unwilling to supply the ruling regime with weapons.[46] Moscow's close relations with New Delhi meant that Russian arms were unavailable, although Russia's increasingly dire economic straits are

---

[42]International Monetary Fund, *Direction of Trade Statistics*, March 1998, p. 52.

[43]Bertil Lintner, "Rangoon's Rubicon," *Far Eastern Economic Review*, February 11, 1993, p. 28.

[44]Stockholm International Peace Research Institute, *SIPRI Yearbook*, 1983–1997 editions.

[45]"Allies in Isolation: Burma and China Move Closer," *Jane's Defence Weekly*, September 15, 1990, p. 475.

[46]In 1991, the European Union banned arms sales to Myanmar. Godemont, "China's Arms Sales," p. 106.

likely to reduce any strategic inhibitions. Myanmar leaders probably also wanted to establish a closer relationship with Beijing to balance the perceived threat from India, because purchasing arms from China gave the impression of Chinese protection of Myanmar.[47] Finally, significantly increased commercial interactions with China since the mid-1980s may have led Yangon to desire improved ties with Beijing.

The most important reasons Myanmar seeks Chinese arms, however, may be that the arms are provided at below-market prices[48] and that they are associated with a broader program of technical and infrastructure assistance from China.[49] In the 1980s, China simply gave some arms to Thailand or else sold them at nominal prices, for geostrategic reasons. It seems plausible that China has been making similar subsidized sales to Myanmar in the 1990s.

Thailand

Thailand received significant amounts of conventional weapons from China in the late 1980s and early 1990s. Many of the weapons were provided as gifts or at extremely low prices. Systems transferred included Type-59 and Type-69 main battle tanks, 130-mm towed artillery, armored personnel carriers, multiple launch rocket systems, HQ-2B and HN-5A surface-to-air missiles, Jianghu-class frigates, and C-801 antishipping missiles.[50]

China's arms transfers to Thailand had two strategic purposes. First, Beijing sought to counter Vietnamese, and by extension Soviet, influ-

---

[47]"One of the attractions of close relations with China from the standpoint of India's smaller neighbors has been their belief that those relations would restrain India and/or mitigate the effects of Indian pressures." John W. Garver, "China-India Rivalry in Nepal: The Clash Over Chinese Arms Sales," *Asian Survey*, Vol. 31, No. 10, October 1991, p. 974.

[48]Bitzinger, "Arms to Go," p. 87.

[49]Chinese radar specialists, engineers, and naval-operations officers have all reportedly been seen at various naval facilities in Myanmar. See Bertil Lintner, "Arms for Eyes," p. 26; Bertil Lintner, ". . . But Stay on Guard," p. 21.

[50]Stockholm International Peace Research Institute, *SIPRI Yearbook*, 1983–1997 editions.

ence in Southeast Asia.[51]   Although the first arms transfers to
Thailand did not occur until 1985, Beijing began making overtures to
Bangkok almost immediately after Vietnam's 1978 invasion of
Cambodia.[52] Transferring arms to Thailand not only strengthened
that country against Vietnamese intimidation, it also served as visible
evidence of China's commitment to Thailand's security, adding
credibility to Beijing's intimations that it would come to Bangkok's
aid in the event of a Vietnamese incursion.   Second, and more
broadly, China's arms transfers to Thailand bolstered Beijing's political influence in Southeast Asia, giving it a role in determining
Cambodia's political future and facilitating the reestablishment of
diplomatic relations between China and Indonesia in 1990.[53]

For its part, Thailand appears to have had several motivations for
purchasing Chinese arms in the 1980s. One was geostrategic. With
Vietnamese forces on Thailand's border, developing close ties to
Beijing helped deter Vietnam from considering attacks on Thailand
at a time when Thailand was providing support and sanctuary for the
Khmer Rouge forces Vietnam was fighting.[54] Beijing also offered an
alternative source for weapon systems, especially when Washington
began to reduce military aid to Thailand after 1986.[55] A final reason
was the extremely low cost of the Chinese equipment. In 1985, China
provided Thailand with artillery and tanks as outright gifts, followed
by transfers of equipment at prices only a fraction of actual value,
with generous repayment terms.[56]

---

[51]Interview at Institute of Asia-Pacific Studies, Shanghai Academy of Social Sciences,
May 1998.

[52]R. Bates Gill, "China Looks to Thailand: Exporting Arms, Exporting Influence," *Asian
Survey,* Vol. 31, No. 6, June 1991, p. 528.

[53]Paisal Sricharatchanya, "'Friendship' Arms Sales," *Far Eastern Economic Review,*
March 19, 1987, p. 15; Gill, "China Looks to Thailand," p. 536.

[54]Rodney Tasker, "Order Arms," *Far Eastern Economic Review,* October 4, 1990, p. 20;
Gill, "China Looks to Thailand," pp. 527–528, 538.

[55]Leszek Buszynski, "New Aspirations and Old Constraints in Thailand's Military
Policy," *Asian Survey,* Vol. 29, No. 11, November 1989, p. 1069; Paisal Sricharatchanya,
"The Chinese Firecracker," *Far Eastern Economic Review,* December 8, 1988, p. 34.

[56]Gill, "China Looks to Thailand," p. 529; Eden Y. Woon, "Chinese Arms Sales and
U.S.-China Military Relations," *Asian Survey,* Vol. 29, No. 6, June 1989, p. 606;
Bitzinger, "Arms to Go," p. 87.

The systems delivered in the 1990s were the result of agreements signed in the late 1980s,[57] and it seems unlikely that Thailand will acquire significant numbers of Chinese weapons in the foreseeable future. Vietnam's withdrawal from Cambodia reduced Thailand's need for a close military relationship with China to deter Vietnam, and Thailand has been dissatisfied with the quality of the Chinese arms it has received. In contrast, the United States has been offering some of its most advanced systems to Thailand.[58] Indeed, the United States agreed to include AMRAAMs (Advanced Medium-Range Air-to-Air Missiles) with F/A-18 fighters it offered in 1997.[59] Finally, Thailand's current financial difficulties will limit its ability to acquire weapons from any country for the next few years.

Thailand's dwindling interest in Chinese arms is reinforced by a decline in interest from Beijing. With the collapse of the Soviet Union and Vietnam's withdrawal from Cambodia, China's strategic interest in supporting Thailand against Vietnam has diminished sharply. Relations with Vietnam have improved markedly and, although Hanoi and Beijing remain suspicious of each other, Vietnam is no longer Beijing's open adversary. Thailand and China no longer need to cooperate in supporting the Cambodian resistance, and Beijing has succeeded in establishing good relations with the Cambodian government. Consequently, the strategic motivation for China's arms sales to Thailand has disappeared and China is unlikely to subsidize further arms sales to that country. Coupled with the Thai dissatisfaction with the arms they have received, this means that future Chinese arms transfers to Thailand are likely to be minimal.

RECIPIENT COUNTRY DEMAND

A great attraction of China's arms has been their price. For example, in 1992 the open-market cost of a Russian MiG-29 was $25 million; the Chinese F-7M sold for $4.5 million at most.[60] Although the F-7M

---

[57]Stockholm International Peace Research Institute, *SIPRI Yearbook*, 1983–1997 editions. The exception is one Similan-class support ship contracted for in 1993.

[58]Tasker, "Order Arms," p. 20.

[59]R. Bates Gill, "Curbing Beijing's Arms Sales," *Orbis*, Summer 1992, p. 384; Rodney Tasker, "Order Arms," p. 20.

[60]Eikenberry, *Explaining and Influencing Chinese Arms Transfers*, p. 34.

is clearly an inferior aircraft, some countries may seek to make up in volume what they lack in quality. Poor countries can more easily build up large militaries using Chinese weapons. Some states have combined small numbers of sophisticated Western systems with large numbers of Chinese systems.[61]

In addition to being inexpensive, Chinese weapons are simple to operate and maintain, a key factor for countries where military professionalism is limited and the technological base is low.[62] The major customers described above are developing countries. The maintenance skills of Iraq, Myanmar, and Pakistan are particularly poor, preventing them from operating Western systems to their full advantage.

Chinese weapons have the additional advantage of being similar to Soviet systems, which form the basis of many developing countries' arsenals. The F-7, for example, is a reverse-engineered MiG-21, and the Type-59 tank is based on the T-54. Countries that are able to operate and maintain older Soviet systems thus are likely to be able to do so with Chinese systems, and many parts and supplies may be interchangeable.

China has also been the only available source of arms for some pariah states, such as Iran and Myanmar, and for certain types of weapons technology for other countries, particularly Pakistan.[63] More generally, Chinese systems allow customers to avoid dependence on the United States and the West and carry few if any political strings.[64] Beijing is often willing to sell arms to countries when Western nations are not.[65] Thus, Saudi Arabia, which faced limits (in the type of systems available and in the systems' use) in sales from the United States because of objections from Israel, bought ballistic missiles from China.[66]

---

[61]Bitzinger, "Arms to Go," p. 92.

[62]Daniel Sneider, "China's Arms Bazaar," *Far Eastern Economic Review*, December 18, 1986, p. 23.

[63]Godemont, "China's Arms Sales," p. 98.

[64]Bitzinger, "Arms to Go," p. 91.

[65]Bitzinger, "Arms to Go," p. 92.

[66]Hyer, "China's Arms Merchants," p. 1106.

In some cases, China has been willing to transfer subsystems and expertise, which is important to countries that wish to build up their own defense industries. Iran, Iraq, Pakistan, and North Korea all benefited from Chinese assistance in developing their own weapons systems.

Several countries have purchased Chinese arms in an attempt to improve political ties to Beijing. Thailand sought Chinese arms in part to gain the imprimatur of Beijing's protection—in effect, conveying the impression to Vietnam that China stood by Bangkok. Myanmar may have taken a similar course beginning in 1989, using its arms relationship with Beijing to send a message to New Delhi.

Despite these attractions, the demand for most Chinese conventional weapons is limited and shrinking. In general, Chinese arms are not sophisticated—the vast majority are clones of old Soviet designs from the 1950s and 1960s—and are of poor quality. The initial Romeo-class submarines China sold to Egypt in 1984 arrived with worn-out engines. Ships sold to the Thai navy had doors that were not watertight and basic mechanical problems.[67] Customers have complained that tank fire-control systems and guns are not stabilized, that the engine quality is poor, and that the steel quality is uncertain.[68] In the Iran-Iraq war, both sides avoided using Chinese systems when possible, relying instead on Western or Soviet systems.[69] Such poor craftsmanship has hurt sales. Customers seeking more sophisticated capabilities will prefer to work with the West or Russia.

Competition has increased since the collapse of the Soviet Union. The price of Russian weapons has plunged, and many states of the former Soviet Union and Eastern Europe are selling their equipment at bargain basement prices. Iran, which was often dissatisfied with Chinese arms, believes Russian ones, suddenly cheaper, provide a

---

[67]Norman Friedman, "Chinese Military Capacity: Industrial and Operational Weaknesses," in *Military Capacity and the Risk of War: China, India, Pakistan, and Iran,* Eric Arnett (ed.), Oxford University Press, New York, 1997, pp. 71–72.

[68]Bitzinger, "Arms to Go," p. 90.

[69]Bitzinger, "Arms to Go," p. 91.

better alternative.[70] As restraints on Russian sales have fallen, developing countries have turned to Moscow for weapons.

Demand for Chinese weapons has also fallen because some of China's best customers are experiencing economic difficulties and thus are unable to purchase more advanced Chinese systems. China has claimed, for example, that Iran's inability to pay led it to stop nuclear cooperation.[71] North Korea has gone from a poor country to an international basket case, reducing its ability to buy any arms. Pakistan's economy has stagnated in recent years, and Myanmar, already one of the poorer countries in Southeast Asia, may be headed for economic collapse.[72]

However, the demand for Chinese weapons could expand. If sanctions are lifted on Iraq, Baghdad may again become a major customer for Beijing. Many of China's transfers have been to one of the most unstable regions of the world—the arc stretching from Pakistan to Egypt. This region is plagued by border disputes, civil wars, and instability in general. The stability of this region will be closely linked to the market for Chinese arms. If turmoil increases, so too will the market for weapons; if stability grows, the demand for arms will shrink. Finally, if China's production capabilities improve, it may find new buyers for its weapons. If China's weapons quality begins to approach that of Russia and the West, its market share will likely increase.

BEIJING'S INCENTIVES

The factors influencing China's arms sales are complex and are not motivated primarily by purely commercial considerations. In almost all cases, a clear political or strategic interest can be associated with China's arms sales to each of its major customers, as demonstrated by the fact that many sales were made at subsidized "friendship" prices. Conversely, in some cases sales have been restricted by polit-

---

[70]Robert Karniol, "China's $4.5b Deal with Iran Cools as Funds Fail," *Jane's Defense Weekly,* August 6, 1997, p. 14.

[71]Kan, *China's Compliance with International Arms Control Agreements*, p. 9.

[72]Shawn W. Crispin, "Heading for a Fall," *Far Eastern Economic Review,* August 27, 1998, p. 56.

ical considerations. Beijing appears to have begun to appreciate the risks of proliferation and wishes to improve its international standing by increasing its commitment to nonproliferation.

This is not to discount commercial motivations in China's arms transfers where Beijing's political interests are limited. For example, the Middle East is far from China and Beijing's interests are primarily economic.[73] However, given the strategic benefits of many sales—and the political costs in terms of damaged relations with the United States—it seems clear that China's arms sales are motivated by strategic and political, not merely commercial, considerations.[74]

China's Foreign Policy Interests

Arms sales serve a wide array of Chinese foreign policy purposes.[75] In many cases, China uses arms transfers to strengthen countries against states that are Beijing's rivals. The transfer of arms to Thailand, Myanmar, and Pakistan strengthened allies against the Soviet Union, Vietnam, and India, respectively. This follows a long-standing pattern dating back to the Sino-Soviet split, when China began selling arms to rivals of Moscow's proxies in the third world.[76] Arms transfers also increase Beijing's strategic reach. For example, China may have supplied Myanmar with advanced radar equipment and other assistance in exchange for access to bases in the Indian Ocean.[77]

China also transfers arms to improve relations with particular countries or regions. Strong ties to Pakistan, for example, facilitate China's relations with countries in the Middle East, giving China influence in this strategically vital region. Similarly, China's transfers of arms to Thailand in the 1980s increased China's influence in Southeast Asia. In some cases, specific political goals may be sought.

---

[73]Authors' interviews at the Institute of West Asian and African Studies, Chinese Academy of Social Sciences, June 1998.

[74]Gill, "Curbing Beijing's Arms Sales," pp. 391–392; Godemont, "China's Arms Sales," pp. 107–108.

[75]Woon, "Chinese Arms Sales," pp. 609–611.

[76]Eikenberry, *Explaining and Influencing Chinese Arms Transfers*, p. 6.

[77]Bertil Lintner, ". . . But Stay on Guard," p. 21.

China's 1987 sale of intermediate-range missiles to Saudi Arabia, for example, apparently contributed to an effort to convince Saudi Arabia to switch recognition from Taipei to Beijing, which Riyadh did in 1990.[78] China may even use the threat of sales to U.S. adversaries as a bargaining chip in its efforts to limit U.S. arms sales to Taiwan.[79]

Given China's growing dependence on imported oil, Chinese analysts have emphasized the importance of maintaining good relations with oil-exporting nations, which may partly explain China's close relations with Iran and its willingness to support the end of Baghdad's isolation.[80] Beijing may hope that these countries will sell China oil on preferential terms or, equally important, will not deny China oil should other oil-producing states, most of which are staunch U.S. allies, embargo China. Such a hope is probably misguided. The world's oil market is advanced, and as many consumers discovered in the 1970s, preferential agreements mean little in the event of a price shock. Nevertheless, even if China's motivations are mistaken, they do shape its arms sales behavior.

Commercial Motivations for Arms Transfers

China's arms sales reflect purely commercial interests along with its foreign policy objectives. At the most basic level, these interests stem largely from China's economic reform program and a decision at the end of the 1970s to reduce the resources being channeled to China's military and defense industries. To compensate for decreased revenues, China's leaders encouraged the defense industries to convert to production of civilian goods and to export both military and civilian products. China's military was encouraged to set up commercial enterprises as a way of generating additional revenues.[81] Although

---

[78]Geoffrey Kemp, *The Control of the Middle East Arms Race*, Carnegie Endowment for International Peace, Washington, 1991, p. 62.

[79]Gill, *Silkworms and Summitry*, p. 21.

[80]Interview at Institute of West Asian and African Studies, Chinese Academy of Social Sciences.

[81]See Eric Arnett, "Military Technology: The Case of China," in Stockholm International Peace Research Institute, *SIPRI Yearbook 1995*, pp. 362–363; James Mulvenon, *Soldiers of Fortune*, Ph.D. Dissertation, University of California at Los Angeles, 1998.

most of the enterprises were not involved in arms production or sales, one People's Liberation Army (PLA)-owned company, Poly Technologies, was heavily engaged in the sale of weapon systems from the PLA inventory (in some cases Poly filled orders by requisitioning newly produced systems that were provided to the PLA at state-subsidized prices and then immediately selling them abroad at international market prices). Selling weapons abroad became an important revenue source for many defense and military organizations.[82]

In addition to providing new sources of revenue for China's military and defense industries, foreign arms sales have provided several other economic benefits to China. During the 1980s, weapons sales constituted a significant source of foreign exchange earnings for China.[83] From 1984 to 1987, when China's arms sales peaked, arms sales produced an estimated $8.2 billion in hard currency for China, equal to about 7 percent of China's total exports during those years. Deng Xiaoping reportedly dismissed the Ministry of Foreign Affairs criticism of the missile sale to Saudi Arabia by asking the leadership of the exporting corporation, "How much money did you make?"[84] The contribution of arms sales to China's total foreign exchange earnings has diminished sharply since that time, however; China's civilian exports have boomed while arms sales have tapered off since the end of the Iran-Iraq war.[85] The value of arms sales in 1996 represented less than 1 percent of China's total exports in that year.[86] China now has over $140 billion in foreign exchange reserves,[87] and it can no longer be argued that China needs to sell weapons to raise hard currency.

---

[82]Hyer, "China's Arms Merchants," p. 1109.

[83]Woon, "Chinese Arms Sales," pp. 607–608.

[84]As quoted in Hyer, "China's Arms Merchants," p. 1106.

[85]China sold over $10 billion in arms to Iran and Iraq throughout the 1980s, fueling the war between the two powers. Hyer, "China's Arms Merchants," p. 1104.

[86]Stockholm International Peace Research Institute, *1997 SIPRI Yearbook*, p. 268; International Monetary Fund, *Direction of Trade Statistics*, March 1998, p. 52.

[87]See for example, "Prices and Trends," *Far Eastern Economic Review*, August 27, 1998, p. 66.

The foreign exchange earned by weapon sales remains significant to China's defense industries and military, however, because they are allowed to retain part of the earnings (another portion goes to the Ministry of Finance).[88]   The PLA's purchases of major imported weapon systems such as Russian Su-27s are reportedly funded by allocations from the central government, so the military's ability to import advanced weapons is not dependent on the hard currency it acquires through its arms sales. However, the foreign exchange generated through these sales may be used to fund the purchases of other scarce imported items.

China's military has other reasons to encourage, or at least to allow, weapons exports. Because much of the cost of producing a weapon system is in the research and development phases, the larger the number of units of a system actually produced, the lower the per-unit cost. In other words, by exporting weapons that are also developed for domestic use, China is effectively using foreigners to help finance its indigenous research and development efforts.[89] In addition, participation in international markets provides a stimulus for technological progress and improvement in the capabilities of China's weapons, since if the systems produced are not competitive, they will not succeed in generating export sales. Also, China may have sold parts of its stockpiles of obsolete weapons. These weapons, intended to defend China's border from Soviet attack, were no longer needed and expensive to maintain. Selling them off aided the PLA's efforts to create a smaller, more sophisticated military.[90]

---

[88]John W. Lewis, Hua Di, and Xue Litai, "Beijing's Defense Establishment: Solving the Arms-Export Enigma," *International Security*, Vol. 15, No. 4, Spring 1991, p. 103.

[89]This approach is not unique to China. The defense industries of many countries, including France and Israel, would not be viable without export markets.

[90]Hyer, "China's Arms Merchants," p. 1111.

Chapter Four

POSSIBLE CONSTRAINTS ON CHINA'S ARMS TRANSFERS

Restrictions imposed by the Chinese central government are the primary nonmarket constraint on China's export of weapons and related systems. The Chinese government might wish to prevent arms sales for three reasons: concern about the effects of weapons proliferation, a desire to adhere to international norms regarding arms transfers, and apprehension about the possible response of specific countries, particularly the United States, to its more controversial arms transfers. The significance of these possible constraints, however, depends on whether the Chinese government actually has control over China's arms transfers: a question we examine next.

BEIJING'S ABILITY TO CONTROL ARMS TRANSFERS

It is sometimes argued that China's central government should not be held responsible for China's arms transfer behavior because sales may take place without Beijing's knowledge or authorization.[1] Although this argument has some validity with regard to various kinds of dual-use equipment and materials, it is not valid with respect to China's sales of actual weapon systems. Most of China's most sensitive arms deals (as opposed to the sales of military-related

---

[1]The Chinese government has *not* made this claim. Indeed, China's official position is that "major transfer items and contracts must be . . . approved by the State Council and the Central Military Commission." State Council of the People's Republic of China, "China: Arms Control and Disarmament," *Beijing Review*, November 27–December 3, 1995, p. 19. See also State Council of the People's Republic of China, "China's National Defense," *Beijing Review*, August 10–16, 1998, p. 34.

technologies and dual-use items) have been conducted by Poly Technologies, which gets approval directly from members of the Central Military Commission (CMC), who are among China's top leaders.[2] Other corporations are authorized to sell less-sophisticated conventional weapons and equipment, but if they wish to sell arms to sensitive regions or to sell more-sophisticated weapons and equipment, they are required to consult with the Ministry of Foreign Affairs (MFA) and other organizations.[3] If the MFA believes that a sale will adversely affect China's foreign relations, it will bring it to the attention of China's top leadership.[4] At times, the MFA's objections are overruled or ignored by the CMC, but this does not mean that the sale in question did not have the approval of the central government. Thus, it is likely that most sensitive weapons sales have occurred with the knowledge and approval of the central government.[5] The argument that China has no control over its arms industries is also undermined by the observation that Chinese arms have not been sold to potential military adversaries, such as Vietnam, India, or Taiwan.[6]

Beijing has argued that it does not control third-party transfers of its equipment.[7] Chinese officials noted, for example, that Iraq in the 1980s bought Chinese arms through Jordan and Egypt and that Iran

---

[2]The Central Military Commission is China's highest military decisionmaking body. As of mid-1999, membership included supreme Chinese leader Jiang Zemin; two retired generals who are also members of the Politburo: Chi Haotian and Zhang Wannian; and the current chiefs of the major departments of the PLA (the General Staff Department, General Logistics Department, and General Political Department), along with the vice-chief of the General Political Department.

[3]However, personal and political networks often allow officials in various trading companies and other sellers to bypass formal approval channels. Wendy Frieman, "China's Defense Industries," *The Pacific Review*, Vol. 6, No. 1, p. 54.

[4]Lewis, Hua, and Xue, "Beijing's Defense Establishment," pp. 93–96. By law the premier is responsible for settling disputes between the MFA and weapons export corporations, although when Yang Shangkun was first vice chairman of the Central Military Commission, Deng Xiaoping (and later Jiang Zemin) apparently deferred to his judgment. *Ibid.*

[5]Again, this argument applies only to weapon systems, not to dual-use materials or technology.

[6]Godemont, "China's Arms Sales," p. 108.

[7]David Bonavia, "Cheap and Deadly," *Far Eastern Economic Review*, May 21, 1987, p. 33; "Who Us?" *Economist*, October 6, 1990, p. 38.

has worked through Pakistan and North Korea.[8] Although technically true, this argument is disingenuous. Beijing could easily influence recipients not to transfer Chinese arms to certain third parties if it so wished. Again, there is no evidence that Chinese arms have made their way to countries that Beijing would be opposed to, such as Vietnam, even though the Vietnamese inventory contains Chinese weapons transferred prior to the 1978 break.[9]

Transfers of dual-use materials and equipment present a different problem. Since the items are not weapons, their export is not channeled through one of the eight or so corporations authorized to conduct arms sales in China. Indeed, in general the transferring entity will have no connection to the military or defense industries.[10] A vast number of enterprises in China engage in export activities, and the system for monitoring and regulating their activities is weak. These enterprises are concerned only with maximizing revenues and are generally uninterested in whether their exports may have military applications. Even if the item they export is explicitly prohibited, the likelihood of the central government's learning of it prior to the sale is low. Limiting China's exports of dual-use goods, therefore, depends on the effectiveness of China's export control system.

China's export control system is just beginning to develop. In September 1997, Beijing announced that it would implement an export license system for nuclear equipment and drew up a list of nuclear materials, equipment, and technologies subject to export controls. In October 1997, China joined the Zangger Committee, which requires that its members allow nuclear exports only to facilities that are safeguarded by the IAEA. In June 1998, China announced export controls on dual-use materials and technology that are comparable to those mandated by the Nuclear Suppliers Group (which China has yet to formally join). To control the export of chemicals, in June 1996

---

[8]Pan Guang, "China's Success in the Middle East," *Middle East Quarterly*, Vol. 4, No. 4, December 1997, p. 38.

[9]International Institute for Strategic Studies, *The Military Balance, 1997/98*, Oxford University Press, London, 1997, pp. 197–198.

[10]This is not true of all dual-use goods, of course. For example, the transfer of ring magnets to Pakistan in 1995–1996 was carried out by the China Nuclear Energy Industry Cooperation, a subsidiary of a firm under the direct control of the State Council, China's cabinet.

China issued a list of chemicals subject to supervision and control and in January 1998 the Chinese media reported that the government had issued instructions requiring a license for the export of chemicals and related technologies.[11] China now prohibits export of 10 of the 24 chemicals banned by the Australia Group (which it also has not yet joined). China has also agreed to conduct regular senior-level dialogues with the United States on arms control and nonproliferation, which should lead to further improvements in its export control system.[12]

Nevertheless, fundamental problems remain. Despite its international pledges and growing commitment to arms control, Beijing still lacks the procedures to effectively implement many agreements. China lacks effective "catch-all" provisions that restrict exports going to potentially sensitive programs. China also lacks well-developed procedures for working with foreign governments that seek to determine the end-use or end-user of systems transferred to China. Moreover, Beijing does not try to go beyond vague assurances from other governments when determining the ultimate destination and use of its exports. China does not share information well within its own government—different regions may not talk to one another or to Beijing, and many companies export without consulting with all the appropriate government agencies.[13] At times, China's commercial interests and international promises conflict, because some Chinese organizations that are responsible for arms control are also tasked with encouraging exports.

Implementing an effective export control system will take time and face many difficulties. The greatest difficulties are likely to be in transparency and verification. The Chinese military in particular is skeptical of transparency, believing that it will give adversaries a future advantage. China also lacks a community well versed in the nuances of arms control.[14]

---

[11]State Council, "China's National Defense," p. 33; "China Clamps Down on Its CW Trading," *Jane's Defense Weekly,* January 7, 1998, p. 5.

[12]Phyllis E. Oakley, Assistant Secretary of State for Intelligence and Research, testimony before the Senate Select Committee on Intelligence, January 28, 1998.

[13]Authors' interviews with U.S. government officials, September 1998.

[14]Authors' interviews conducted at the Institute of American Studies, Beijing, May 1998.

BEIJING'S ATTITUDES TOWARD ARMS SALES AND PROLIFERATION

Until recently, China's leadership has shown little concern for the dangers of proliferation of nuclear, biological, and chemical weapons, the spread of ballistic missiles, and transfers of certain types of conventional weapons to unstable regions or regimes. In recent years, however, there have been indications that the attitudes of China's leadership are beginning to change, which could act as a restraint on future dangerous arms transfers by China.

Prior to 1982, China officially opposed the idea of nuclear nonproliferation.[15] Although China finally declared its support for the principle of nonproliferation in 1982, it nevertheless directly aided Pakistan's nuclear program throughout the 1980s. It also provided assistance to nuclear programs in Algeria and Iran. Although this latter assistance was technically consistent with the NPT, which China signed in 1992, and was conducted under IAEA safeguards, China's leadership can have had few illusions about their assistance contributing to efforts by those two countries to develop nuclear weapons.

However, in October 1997, China promised to end its nuclear cooperation with Iran, reportedly in part because China recognized that Iranian-sponsored instability in the Gulf could jeopardize China's energy security.[16] Nuclear weapons tests in May 1998 by China's neighbors India and Pakistan appear to have further awakened China's leaders to the dangers of nuclear proliferation. Interviews in China in June 1998 indicated concern that the Indian and Pakistani tests might legitimize tests by countries of more direct concern to China, such as Korea, Japan, or Taiwan.[17] At their summit in June,

---

[15]Zachary S. Davis, "China's Nonproliferation and Export Control Policies," *Asian Survey*, Vol. 35, No. 6, June 1995, pp. 588–591. Opposition was on the grounds that it was discriminatory in favor of the existing nuclear weapons states. This view is still espoused in mainland-backed publications. See Chao Ching-tseng, Pan Chu-sheng, and Liu Hua-ch'iu, "Analysis of Situation in World Arms Control, Disarmament," *Hsien-tai Chun-shih (Conmilit)*, No. 230, March 6, 1996, pp. 15–16 in *Foreign Broadcast Information Service, Daily Report: China*, March 6, 1996.

[16]"A New China Embracing Nuclear Nonproliferation," p. 1.

[17]Interviews with researchers at the Chinese Academy of Social Sciences and China Institute for Contemporary International Relations, June 1998. Also see Andrew Mack,

Presidents Clinton and Jiang issued a joint statement in which they pledged to "prevent the export of equipment, materials, or technology that could in any way assist programs in India or Pakistan for nuclear weapons."[18]

Chinese attitudes toward proliferation of chemical and biological weapons may also be changing. Although China signed the Biological Warfare Convention (BWC) in 1984 and the Chemical Weapons Convention (CWC) in 1993, it has continued to export equipment and materials to Iran that could be used to manufacture biological and chemical weapons, despite evidence that they probably are being used by Iran's chemical and biological warfare programs. On the other hand, China has not exported actual chemical or biological weapons technology, despite believed capability in both areas. China has strengthened its controls over chemical exports in recent years, however, and at the Clinton-Jiang summit in June 1998 Beijing agreed to further strengthen its export controls.[19] Whether this reflects a change in attitude with regard to the dangers of spreading chemical and biological weapons or is merely a response to U.S. pressure is unclear.

China has been resistant to the idea that transfers of missiles represent a danger qualitatively different from other conventional arms transfers. From Beijing's viewpoint, missiles are simply a delivery system no different from conventional aircraft (e.g., the F-16s the United States has sold to Taiwan), which have a greater range and payload than many missiles banned under the Missile Technology Control Regime (MTCR).[20] Beijing therefore sees the MTCR as sim-

---

Proliferation in Northeast Asia, Henry L. Stimson Center, Washington DC, 1996, pp. 5–6.

[18]Quoted in Susan V. Lawrence, "Sparring Partners," *Far Eastern Economic Review*, July 9, 1998, p. 13. However, China is apparently not ready to play an active role in preventing the spread of dangerous arms. Despite concern about the spread of NBC and missiles in Asia—particularly in India—Chinese interlocutors in interviews conducted at Chinese research institutions in May-June 1998, could think of no way that China would aid U.S. initiatives to control their spread beyond vague promises of diplomatic support. Economic sanctions were rejected for a variety of reasons, ranging from their limited impact to China's "tradition" of non-interference in other countries' affairs.

[19]Lawrence, "Sparring Partners," p. 13.

[20]Wolfsthal, Jon Brook, "U.S. and Chinese Views on Proliferation: Trying to Bridge the Gap," *The Nonproliferation Review*, Fall 1994, p. 61.

ply promoting the interests of advanced military powers such as the United States, which are able to defend themselves against air attacks but not against missile attacks.[21] Indeed, Chinese leaders may suspect that the MTCR was directed specifically against China.[22] Thus, while China has agreed, under U.S. pressure, to adhere to the guidelines of the MTCR, it has not formally joined the regime, which may suggest continuing opposition to the principle of nonproliferation of missiles. More important, Beijing has had no reservations about providing technical assistance to missile programs in Iran and Pakistan that are ostensibly for systems that fall below the MTCR threshold, despite the fact that this assistance undoubtedly aids other ballistic missile programs in both countries. At the Clinton-Jiang summit, China announced that it was "actively considering" joining the MTCR,[23] but whether this statement was simply a way of deflating American pressure on the subject or instead reflected changing attitudes about the dangers of missile proliferation is not clear. Until these attitudes change, concern about the dangers of missile proliferation is not likely to restrain China's transfers of missiles and related technology.

Beijing claims it already restricts its transfers of conventional arms. In 1988, China announced "three principles" for its arms sales: strengthening the buyer's legitimate self-defense needs, safeguarding peace and stability in the regions concerned, and not using military sales to interfere with the internal affairs of other states. These principles are vague and subjective, and in any case Beijing has clearly not always adhered to them. China has sold arms to highly unstable regions, such as the Persian Gulf, has supplied aggressive regimes such as Iraq, and has aided insurgents in countries such as Cambodia.[24] China also resists the idea that individual countries

---

[21]Robert E. Mullins, "The Dynamics of Chinese Missile Proliferation," pp. 153–155; Roxane D.V. Sisimandis, "The Paradoxes of Asian Security," *The China Business Review*, November–December 1995, pp. 10–11. Another reason given for opposition to the MTCR is that China was not involved in creation of the regime. Wolfsthal, "U.S. and Chinese Views on Proliferation," p. 61.

[22]Godemont, "China's Arms Sales," p. 105.

[23]Lawrence, "Sparring Partners," p. 13.

[24]Chinese leaders have argued that weapon sales to volatile regions (such as the Persian Gulf in the 1980s) can actually contribute to stability by ensuring a military stalemate. Cheung, "Proliferation Is Good, and There's Money in It Too," pp. 27–28.

such as Iran should be subject to weapons embargoes. Nonetheless, there appears to be some recognition in Beijing that certain conventional weapons transfers can be destabilizing.[25]

China's Degree of Adherence to Nonproliferation Regimes

Prior to 1992, the only nonproliferation treaty China was a party to was the Biological Warfare Convention, which it joined in 1984. Since 1992, however, China has joined most remaining major nonproliferation regimes. In 1992, China signed the NPT, in 1993 it joined the Chemical Weapons Convention, and in 1996 it signed the Comprehensive Test Ban Treaty (CTBT). China also joined the Zangger Committee (although not the Nuclear Suppliers Group) in 1997.[26] In addition, in 1992 China agreed bilaterally with the United States to adhere to the 1987 parameters of the MTCR. Since these regimes address many of the types of weapons considered most dangerous, the extent to which China actually abides by the rules will largely determine the degree to which it engages in dangerous arms transfers.

The decision to participate in international arms control regimes apparently reflects a judgment by China's leadership that the costs of openly refusing to adhere to international nonproliferation norms exceed the costs of accepting them. This decision may have been part of an effort to reduce China's isolation and improve its image after the 1989 Tiananmen killings. In any case, China's leaders evidently want to be viewed as abiding by these regimes. Thus, any accusations of violations produce vigorous denials and legalistic defenses. Nonetheless, as Beijing's ambivalence toward restrictions on arms transfers would suggest, China's adherence to these regimes is imperfect. In addition, China has violated the spirit of the regimes

---

[25]For example, "China . . . is very concerned about the adverse effects on world security and regional stability arising from excessive accumulations of weaponry." State Council, "China: Arms Control and Disarmament," p. 19.

[26]Mitchel B. Wallerstein, "China and Proliferation: A Path Not Taken?" *Survival*, Vol. 38, No. 3, Autumn 1996, p. 60; Kan, *China's Compliance with International Arms Control Agreements*, pp. 6–9. China is the only major nuclear supplier that is not a member of the Nuclear Suppliers Group, which requires that its members provide nuclear assistance only to those countries that have accepted IAEA safeguards on all facilities in the country ("full-scope safeguards").

by engaging in transfers which, if not necessarily explicitly banned, contradict the intent.

Although China has often violated the spirit of its nonproliferation commitments, there are relatively few instances of China violating the exact letter of these agreements.[27] The one publicly known possible violation of the NPT by China was its 1995 transfer of ring magnets to an unsafeguarded facility in Pakistan, which in the opinion of some experts violated the NPT, because the magnets represented "equipment or material especially designed or prepared for the processing, use or production" of fissionable materials to facilities not under IAEA safeguards.[28] This opinion was based on the argument that the ring magnets had no application other than in centrifuges used to make enriched uranium. However, because ring magnets do not appear on international lists for nuclear export controls (such as the IAEA Trigger List), it is possible that Chinese officials, although knowing full well what the magnets were to be used for, did not believe that they violated the NPT.[29] In May 1996, China pledged not to assist unsafeguarded nuclear facilities and it has not been accused of doing so since.[30]

Similarly, although the United States imposed sanctions on two private Chinese companies in 1997 for assisting Iran's chemical weapons program, Beijing has not been accused of knowingly violating the Chemical Weapons Convention.[31] China has been accused of exporting chemicals and equipment that can be used in the development of chemical or biological weapons, but these materials are not specifically banned by the CWC or BWC.

---

[27]"China's Broken Promises," *Economist,* July 8, 1995, pp. 17–18.

[28]Subcommittee on International Security, Proliferation, and Federal Services, *The Proliferation Primer,* pp. 4-6.

[29]"Row Over?" *Economist,* May 18, 1996, p. 37. Ring magnets are a component of magnetic suspension bearings used in gas centrifuges, which are on the Trigger List. Shirley A. Kan, *China's Compliance with International Arms Control Agreements,* p. 7.

[30]Subcommittee on International Security, Proliferation, and Federal Services, *The Proliferation Primer,* pp. 5–6, 9–10.

[31]In May 1997, the United States imposed sanctions on two Chinese companies and five Chinese individuals for knowingly assisting Iran's chemical weapons program. The two companies were not state-owned. Subcommittee on Security, Proliferation, and Federal Services, *The Proliferation Primer,* p. 8.

China did apparently violate the MTCR (which it has not formally joined but whose guidelines it has promised to abide by) when it transferred components of M-11 missiles to Pakistan in November 1992. Beijing argued that since the M-11 has a range of only 280 km, it did not violate the MTCR, which prohibits the transfer of missiles capable of carrying 500 kg to a range of 300 km or more. The U.S. position was that, since the M-11 has a payload of 800 kg, by reducing the payload the M-11 could be modified to carry 500 kg over 300 km and thus exceeded the MTCR parameters. The Chinese government may well have been acting in bad faith when it transferred M-11 missiles to Pakistan, but it may have done so in the belief that the M-11 technically did not violate the MTCR, or at least that it could credibly make such an argument. It is noteworthy, for example, that the system in dispute is the M-11 and not the M-9, which, with its 600-km range, clearly would violate the MTCR, despite the fact that the M-9 was originally developed for export.[32]

The Chinese government ultimately accepted the "inherent capabilities" argument in a subsequent agreement with the United States reached in October 1994 and does not appear to have engaged in further violations since this agreement. Iran's recent development of an intermediate range missile, for example, is apparently based primarily on North Korean No Dong technology, not a Chinese system, despite previous reports that China and Iran were jointly developing a 1000-km solid-fuel missile.[33] Other U.S. complaints have focused on the transfer of subsystems and technology, violations of Category II of the MTCR guidelines, which China has not explicitly committed to upholding. Thus, although Beijing remains skeptical of the MTCR, it appears to be abiding by its pledges on missile transfers.

China may become more accepting of international regimes. Several Chinese analysts have noted that the coming generation of Chinese leaders is less inclined to view international relations in "zero-sum" terms and is less hostile toward U.S. dominance.[34] As described

---

[32]Bates Gill, "Curbing Beijing's Arms Sales."

[33]Walter Pincus, "Iran May Soon Gain Missile Capability," *Washington Post*, July 24, 1998, p. A28; Duncan Lennox (ed.), *Jane's Strategic Weapon Systems*, Issue 18, May 1995.

[34]Authors' interviews at the Center for American Studies, Fudan University, Shanghai, May 1998.

below, constant U.S. pressure may also be taking its toll, leading Chinese elites to recognize that even the sale of relatively small numbers of arms damages relations with the United States—perhaps China's most important foreign policy concern. In addition, China's leaders may come to regard proliferation as no longer in China's interests, particularly when the countries in question—Iran, Pakistan, and North Korea—are all in close proximity to China.

The positive trend in China's recent proliferation behavior could, of course, reverse in the coming years. If relations with the United States deteriorate, sales could increase if Beijing no longer sees value in appeasing Washington. Proliferation by others could also increase Chinese sales. Part of China's recent improvement in its proliferation behavior stems from its reluctance to be isolated. If it found that others were transferring sophisticated technologies, Beijing would have fewer inhibitions in doing so as well. Barring such developments, however, China is likely to continue or even increase its commitment to international arms control regimes.

U.S. Ability to Influence Beijing

The United States and other nations can influence China's proliferation behavior. Perhaps the greatest point of leverage is that China's leaders clearly wish for China to be seen as a responsible member of the international community and recognize that open violations of nonproliferation agreements undermine this image. China has not sold arms to Iraq in violation of the UN embargo, for example, despite having a long-established military relationship with Baghdad.[35] In addition to appealing to Beijing's desire to be seen as a responsible power, the United States has various foreign policy tools, including access to U.S. technology, to influence China's arms sales behavior. Restrictions on transfers of U.S. technology led China to suspend—albeit temporarily—sales of antishipping cruise missiles to Iran in 1988 and to agree to adhere to the MTCR in 1992 and 1994. Similarly, in October 1997 Beijing pledged to end its nuclear assis-

---

[35]Alexander T. Lennon, "Trading Guns, Not Butter," *The China Business Review*, March–April 1994, p. 48.

tance to Iran partly because the United States said it would end its ban on sales of nuclear power technology to China.[36]

Pressure from the United States and others has prevented arms transfers in a number of other instances. China's leaders recognize that arms transfers to countries such as Iran affect China's relationships with the United States and other major countries.[37] Israel was apparently able to prevent the transfer of M-9 missiles to Syria, and U.S. pressure may have led China to cancel an agreement to transfer M-11 missiles to Iran in 1991 and again in 1992.[38] In 1995, U.S. lobbying may have led China to cancel its plan to provide a complete nuclear reactor to Iran, even though this transfer was legal under the NPT and Zangger Committee provisions. In January 1998, Defense Secretary William Cohen indicated that Beijing had assured Washington that China would not transfer more antishipping missiles to Iran.[39]

U.S. pressure, on top of Beijing's general desire to be seen as a responsible power, has also resulted in China's increasing its membership in, and compliance with, international nonproliferation regimes, despite its initial opposition to the nonproliferation norm. U.S. pressure, for example, led China to pledge in 1992 to abide by the MTCR. When the United States objected to China's transfer of M-11 missiles to Pakistan, China agreed to clarify its commitment to include the M-11. In 1996, U.S. pressure caused China to promise not to assist unsafeguarded nuclear facilities and in 1997 and 1998 to announce more-comprehensive export control regulations.

However, Beijing's track record of actually implementing its promises on arms transfers is mixed. In March 1988, for example, China pledged that it would not sell Iran more antiship cruise mis-

---

[36]Subcommittee on International Security, Proliferation, and Federal Services, *The Non-Proliferation Primer*, p. 10. This leverage was particularly effective because Congress was also considering increasing restrictions on technology flows to China if Beijing did not limit its cooperation with Iran.

[37]Israel, for example, is one of China's most important sources of advanced military technology.

[38]Godemont, "China's Arms Sales," pp. 103–104; Gill, *Silkworms and Summitry*, p. 10.

[39]Kan, *Chinese Proliferation of Weapons of Mass Destruction: Current Policy Issues*, p. 6.

siles. In fact, after 1990, China began providing Iran with more-advanced C-801 and C-802 antishipping missiles.[40] In addition, in the early 1990s, China reportedly helped Iran with indigenous production of the HY-2 Silkworm and may now be helping Iran indigenously produce a medium-range antiship missile, the FL-10, which is based on Chinese designs.[41] These latter actions are reflective of a general pattern—after promising to refrain from sales of a particular system, Beijing has instead provided know-how and technical assistance. Despite stopping sales of the M-9 and M-11 missiles to Iran after U.S. objections, for example, Beijing has provided production equipment, expertise, and technology that have contributed to Iran's indigenous missile development programs.[42] Similarly, despite China's agreement not to transfer M-11 missile technology to Pakistan, missile technicians and missile-related equipment reportedly continued to travel between China and Pakistan through 1997.[43]

From Beijing's perspective, the United States also has not carried out the spirit of its agreements with China regarding arms sales. In the "August 17" communiqué of 1982, the United States pledged that "its arms sales to Taiwan will not exceed, either in qualitative or quantitative terms, the level of those supplied in recent years."[44] In fact, although sales of complete systems to Taiwan have gradually decreased since 1982, this decrease has been more than made up for by transfers of military technology in what one Western observer has described as "a sort of technology laundering scheme."[45] In addition, in 1992 the United States decided to sell F-16s to Taiwan in what Beijing viewed as a violation of Washington's commitment to

---

[40]Gill, *Silkworms and Summitry*, p. 7.

[41]Gill, *Silkworms and Summitry*, p. 9.

[42]Gill, *Silkworms and Summitry*, p. 11.

[43]Gary Milhollin, Testimony before the Senate Intelligence Committee, September 18, 1997.

[44]See, for example, Stephen Friedman and Elizabeth Economy, *Managing the Taiwan Issue: Key Is Better U.S. Relations with China*, Council on Foreign Relations, New York, 1995, p. 48.

[45]Eric Arnett, "Military Research and Development," in Stockholm International Peace Research Institute, *SIPRI Yearbook 1997*, p. 235.

the August 17 communiqué.[46] As long as Beijing perceives Washington as carrying out the letter but not the spirit of its own bilateral commitments, China is likely to do so as well.

A lack of allied support weakens U.S. pressure on China. So far, the United States stands alone in taking action to prevent the spread of missile and nuclear technologies by China to Iran. Unless the United States has a monopoly on a technology, the effectiveness of policy tools such as restricting access to key technologies is thus limited. U.S. ability to influence China's (and other countries') arms transfers would be greatly enhanced if other industrial countries would form a united front with the United States to withhold access to markets or technology if China persists in carrying out particularly threatening transfers.

---

[46]The F-5 was the most advanced aircraft the United States had previously sold to Taiwan. Washington argued that, since the F-5 was no longer produced, the F-16 was the closest equivalent of aircraft previously supplied to Taiwan.

Chapter Five

IMPLICATIONS FOR THE UNITED STATES

China's arms sales are a significant, though manageable, problem for the United States. Beijing's transfers have increased the strength and autonomy of pariah states and helped missile and NBC systems spread, although Beijing in recent years has been less supportive of pariah states and more responsible in its NBC-related transfers. Despite these improvements, further progress is necessary before China's behavior stops posing a threat to U.S. interests.

Our analysis supports three significant findings about China's arms sales behavior. First, the claim that China's arms transfers are motivated primarily by the desire to generate export earnings is inaccurate. In fact, virtually all of China's arms transfers are at least partly driven by foreign policy considerations, and revenues from arms sales are of diminishing importance to Beijing. Second, the related claim that China's central government has only a limited ability to control arms transfers is also inaccurate. China's weapons export system is in fact quite centralized, with the most sensitive transfers of complete systems requiring the approval of a member of the Central Military Commission—comparable to requiring the approval of a member of the U.S. Joint Chiefs of Staff or the National Security Council.[1] The third conclusion is more positive from a U.S. perspective: China's adherence to international nonproliferation norms is in fact increasing. China has joined several international nonproliferation regimes since 1992, including the Non-Proliferation

---

[1]Note that this statement applies only to complete weapon systems, not dual-use materials and equipment.

Treaty, Chemical Weapons Convention, and Zangger Committee, and has not egregiously violated any of the regimes it has formally joined.[2] In addition, there are signs that Beijing intends to comply with or even join the Missile Technology Control Regime and the Nuclear Suppliers Group.

However, China has a long road to travel before its behavior meets U.S. standards:

- Beijing has not completely accepted the norms embodied in some arms control regimes, and thus often reverts to excessive legalism when interpreting its obligations, using any loopholes in an opportunistic fashion to continue transfers.

- The central government's ability to monitor and control transfers of dual-use materials and equipment is currently limited, in contrast to its control over transfers of actual weapon systems. It is logistically difficult to monitor over $100 billion in manufactured exports annually in an increasingly decentralized economy with a poorly developed legal system. Beijing also lacks experience and expertise in implementing a monitoring system.

- China's commitment to the Missile Technology Control Regime is weaker than its commitment to other nonproliferation regimes.

- China is likely to remain resistant to the idea that it should refrain from transfers of certain types of conventional arms because of concerns about the nature of the recipient regime. For example, although China has reportedly agreed not to make further transfers of antishipping missiles to Iran, it remains to be seen whether China accepts as a general principle that it should not sell certain types of conventional weapons to countries like Iran.

---

[2]China is, however, suspected of maintaining its own chemical weapons program in violation of the CWC. Office of the Secretary of Defense, *Proliferation: Threat and Response*, Washington DC, November 1997, p. 9.

IMPLICATIONS OF UNPREVENTABLE TRANSFERS

Although the United States has some ability to inhibit China's most worrisome arms transfers, some transactions will inevitably occur. The U.S. focus should continue to be on NBC and missile systems, particularly technology transfers. Transfers of conventional weapons—even to rogues—are far less of a problem given the unsophisticated nature of most Chinese conventional weapons.

China's transfers of conventional weapons are likely to continue at the reduced levels they have sustained since the late 1980s.[3] China's principal customers in the 1990s have been Iran, Myanmar, and Pakistan, and this is likely to remain true for the foreseeable future, although these countries are suffering from economic stagnation (at best) and are not likely to increase arms purchases dramatically. Because Chinese conventional weapon systems—combat aircraft, main battle tanks, and air-to-air and surface-to-air missiles—are unsophisticated, they do not present major challenges to U.S. military capabilities. The principal concern has been China's antishipping missiles, which threaten unarmed merchant vessels such as oil tankers. Nonetheless, Chinese transfers of conventional weapons could threaten U.S. interests by altering regional balances of power or precipitating a conflict into which the United States is drawn.

Of most concern are transfers of nuclear weapons technology. Although it is possible that China may continue assistance to Pakistan's nuclear weapons program, it is unlikely to directly assist the nuclear weapons programs of any other country. It may do so indirectly by providing assistance to civilian research and nuclear power programs. This latter type of assistance would not be in violation of China's obligations as a member of the Non-Proliferation Treaty or Zangger Committee, although it is possible that some dual-use equipment and materials may be sold without the approval of the central government. China also appears to be committed to refraining from transferring chemical weapons abroad, although again, especially given the size of China's chemical industry and the relatively basic nature of chemical weapons technology, some dual-use equipment and materials are likely to escape export controls. In

---

[3]See Stockholm International Peace Research Institute, *SIPRI Yearbook 1995*, p. 441.

sum, China's transfers of nuclear and chemical equipment and technology greatly aided Pakistan's nuclear weapons program and may well contribute to further improvements in Pakistan's capabilities. In addition, China's arms transfers will probably make a minor contribution to Iran's efforts to develop nuclear and chemical weapons. Furthermore, both Pakistan and Iran could pass these technologies on to other countries. The likelihood that the United States Air Force could become involved in a conflict with an adversary possessing nuclear or chemical weapons is therefore increased.

The missile technology that China has transferred to Pakistan and Iran is another serious concern. The M-series of missiles represent a qualitative improvement over the Scud missiles common in Third World inventories. They are longer range, more accurate, mobile, and, because they are solid-fueled, can be ready to fire much more quickly. If this technology spread to countries that are adversaries of the United States, it would present serious difficulties for U.S. military planners. Even if China does not specifically transfer M-series missile technology, its other transfers of missile-related technology are of concern. Iran's Shahab-3 medium-range missile, for example, which is based on the far cruder North Korean No Dong, may have benefited from Chinese guidance technology.[4] Although China's outright missile sales have been restrained, the United States Air Force must nonetheless prepare for the possibility that potential regional adversaries such as Iran will be equipped with Chinese missile technology.

FINAL WORDS

China's arms sales will make the future security environment more dangerous. Although Beijing's behavior is improving, continued pressure is necessary to minimize China's most dangerous sales, particularly those to rogue regimes. China has been, and can be, influenced by U.S. pressure, although some level of sales is likely to continue. Thus, Washington must hedge against the likelihood of sales, developing offsets in concert with allies to minimize danger.

---

[4]Pincus, "Iran May Soon Gain Missile Capability," p. A28.

AN OVERVIEW OF CHINA'S ARMS SALES

This appendix lists China's transfers of weapon systems since 1980. The data in the table carry several caveats. First, they represent reported sales either declared by the governments in question or uncovered by the media. Sales of more sensitive items, such as chemical, biological, and nuclear materials and missiles, often take place in considerable secrecy. Thus, the table below may underrepresent sensitive sales. Second, the table does not list transfers of subcomponents or expertise. Such transfers, as noted above, may be more dangerous in the long term than transfers of a complete system. China's NBC and missile transfers generally fall into this category. Third, many of China's most important customers—Iran, Iraq, North Korea, and Myanmar in particular—are highly secretive and do not report fully (or at all) on many transfers.

Recipient	Weapon/System	Delivery Year (s)	Quantity
Afghanistan	Hong Ying-5 portable surface-to-air missile (SAM)	1982–89	850
Afghanistan	Type-63 107mm MRL (multiple rocket launcher)	1982–89	350
Algeria	Hainan-class patrol craft	1990	4
Bangladesh	A5-A Fantan-A fighter	1989–90	20
Bangladesh	A5-C Fantan fighter/ground attack	1989–90	20
Bangladesh	BT-6 trainer	1979–85	38
Bangladesh	F-6 fighter	1992	40
Bangladesh	F-7 fighter	1989	16
Bangladesh	F-7M airguard fighter	1989	21
Bangladesh	Fei Lung ShShM	1989–90	8

Recipient	Weapon/System	Delivery Year (s)	Quantity
Bangladesh	Hai Ying-2 ShShM	1989	12
Bangladesh	Hai Ying-2-L ShShM launcher	1989	1
Bangladesh	Hainan-class fast attack craft	1984	3
Bangladesh	Hainan-class patrol craft	1982–85	2
Bangladesh	Huangfen fast attack craft (FAC)	1988, 1992	5
Bangladesh	Huchuan fast attack craft	1988	4
Bangladesh	HY-2 ship-to-ship missile	1988–89, 1992	64
Bangladesh	HY-2 ship-to-ship missile system	1988–89, 1992	6
Bangladesh	Jianghu-class frigate	1989–90	2
Bangladesh	Romeo-class submarine	1984	1
Bangladesh	Square Tie surveillance radar	1989	1
Bangladesh	T-43-class minesweeper	1995–96	2
Bangladesh	T-62 light tank	1985	36
Cambodia	Hong Ying-5 portable SAM	1988	20
Cambodia	HY-5A portable SAM	1988	20
Cambodia	T-59 main battle tank	1990	24
Cambodia	T-60 122mm towed gun	1988	6
Chile	Hong Jian-73 antitank missile	1988	60
Chile	Red Arrow 8 antitank missile	1988	10
Egypt	F-7 fighter	1982–86	80
Egypt	Hai Ying-2 ShShM/SShM	1984	96
Egypt	Hainan-class fast attack craft	1983–84	7
Egypt	Huangfen fast attack craft	1984	6
Egypt	Jianghu-class frigate	1984–85	3
Egypt	Romeo-class submarine	1982–85	6
Guinea-Bissau	Type-55 APC	1984	20
Iran	C-801 ShShM	1987	100
Iran	C-801 ShShM launcher	1987	8
Iran	C-802 ship-to-ship missile	1994–96	80
Iran	C-802 ship-to-ship missile system	1994–96	10
Iran	CSA-1 SAM	1985–86	130
Iran	CSA-1 SAM system	1985–86	6
Iran	ESR-1 surveillance radar	1994–96	10
Iran	F-6 fighter	1982–88	93
Iran	F-7 fighter	1986–88	44
Iran	F-7M airguard fighter	1992–94	68
Iran	Hai Ying-2-L ShShM launcher	1987–88	8
Iran	Hai Ying-2 ShShM/SShM	1987–88	124
Iran	Hong Jian-73 antitank missile	1982–88	6,500
Iran	Hong Ying-5 portable SAM	1985–88	600
Iran	HQ-2B SAM	1990–93	96

Recipient	Weapon/System	Delivery Year (s)	Quantity
Iran	HQ-2B SAM system	1990–93	8
Iran	Hudong-class fast attack craft (M)	1994–96	10
Iran	Oghab SSM (surface-to-surface missile)	1986–91	1,000
Iran	PL-2A AAM	1986–88	540
Iran	PL-7 AAM	1986–88	360
Iran	Rice Lamp fire control radar	1994–96	10
Iran	T-59 main battle tank	1982–88	740
Iran	Type 501 APC	1986–88	300
Iran	Type 59/1 130mm towed gun	1982–87	520
Iran	Type 60 122mm towed gun	1985–86	100
Iran	Type 63 MRL	1983–90	800
Iraq	B-6 bomber	1988	4
Iraq	C-601 antiship missile	1988	128
Iraq	Hai Ying-2 ShShM/SShM	1987	72
Iraq	T-59 main battle tank	1982–88	700
Iraq	T-69 main battle tank	1983–88	600
Iraq	Type 531 APC	1982–88	650
Iraq	Type 59/1 130mm towed gun	1982–88	720
Laos	Y-12 transport aircraft	1990	2
Myanmar	A-5C Fantan/ fighter/ground attack	1996	12
Myanmar	A-5M fighter/ground attack	1995	12
Myanmar	F-6 fighter	1990–91	24
Myanmar	F-7 fighter	1990–91	6
Myanmar	F-7M airguard fighter	1990–95	29
Myanmar	FT-7 fighter trainer	1990–95	6
Myanmar	Hainan-class patrol craft	1991–93	10
Myanmar	HY-5A portable SAM	1991–92	200
Myanmar	JY-8A fire control radar	1993	1
Myanmar	PL-2A air-to-air missile (AAM)	1990–92	48
Myanmar	PL-2B AAM	1990–96	120
Myanmar	T-311 fire control radar	1993	6
Myanmar	T-62 light tank	1989–90, 1993	105
Myanmar	T-63 107mm MRL	1993	30
Myanmar	T-63 light tank	1989–90	50
Myanmar	T-69 main battle tank	1990	50
Myanmar	T-69-II main battle tank	1990, 1995	80
Myanmar	Y-12 transport aircraft	1991	1
Myanmar	Y-8 transport aircraft	1992–93	2
Myanmar	YW-531H armored personnel carrier (APC)	1993	150

Recipient	Weapon/System	Delivery Year (s)	Quantity
Nepal	P-793 AAV (antiaircraft vehicle, gun-armed)	1988	10
North Korea	F-6 fighter	1982–89	144
North Korea	HN-5A portable SAM	1983–94	600
North Korea	HY-2 ship-to-ship missile	1977–89	156
North Korea	Romeo-class submarine	1975–92	15
North Korea	T-63 107mm MRL	1982–85	100
North Yemen	F-7 fighter	1989	6
Pakistan	A-5 Fantan-A fighter	1986–88	98
Pakistan	Anza portable SAM	1989–93	450
Pakistan	Anza-2 SAM	1989–96	750
Pakistan	CSA-1 SAM	1985	20
Pakistan	F-7 fighter	1986–90	75
Pakistan	F-7M airguard fighter	1993	20
Pakistan	F-7MP airguard	1985–93	120
Pakistan	FT-7/FT-7P trainer	1987, 1991	19
Pakistan	Fuqing-class support ship	1987	1
Pakistan	Hai Ying-2 ShShM/SShM	1984	16
Pakistan	HJ-8 antitank missile	1990–93	200
Pakistan	HN-5A portable SAM	1989–90	200
Pakistan	Hoku class FAC	1980	2
Pakistan	Hong Ying-5 portable SAM	1988–90	300
Pakistan	Huangfen-class FAC	1984	4
Pakistan	K-8 Karakorum-8 jet trainer aircraft	1994–96	30
Pakistan	Khalid main battle tank (based on T-69?)	1991	10
Pakistan	M-11 surface-to-surface missile	1991	55
Pakistan	M-11 surface-to-surface missile system	1991	20
Pakistan	P-58A patrol craft	1987–90	4
Pakistan	Q-5 Fantan-A fighter/ground attack	1982–87	148
Pakistan	Red Arrow 8 antitank missile	1990–93	200
Pakistan	T-59 main battle tank	1977–90	987
Pakistan	T-69 main battle tank	1989–91	275
Pakistan	T-69-II main battle tank	1991–95	339
Pakistan	T-85 main battle tank	1993	12
Pakistan	T-85-II-AP main battle tank	1992–95	282
Peru	Y-12 transport aircraft	1991	6
Romania	Huchuan-class hydrofoil fast attack craft	1974–1983	17
Saudi Arabia	CSS-2 IRBM (intermediate range BM)	1987–88	50
Sri Lanka	F-7 fighter	1991	4
Sri Lanka	F-7BS fighter	1991	5
Sri Lanka	FT-5 jet trainer	1991	2
Sri Lanka	Shanghai-class patrol craft	1991	3

Recipient	Weapon/System	Delivery Year (s)	Quantity
Sri Lanka	T-59-1 130mm towed gun	1991	12
Sri Lanka	WZ-551 infantry fighting vehicle	1991	10
Sri Lanka	Y-12 transport aircraft	1986–89, 1991	9
Sri Lanka	Y-8 transport aircraft	1989, 1993	4
Sri Lanka	YW-531 APC	1991–92	20
Sudan	F-7M airguard fighter	1996	6
Sudan	Y-8 transport aircraft	1991	2
Thailand	C-801 ship-to-ship missile	1991–92	96
Thailand	C-801 ship-to-ship missile system	1991–92	4
Thailand	Hong Ying-5 portable SAM	1988	18
Thailand	HQ-2B SAM	1989	12
Thailand	HQ-2B SAM system	1989	1
Thailand	HY-5A portable SAM	1987–88	68
Thailand	Jianghu-class frigate	1991–92	4
Thailand	Naresuan-class frigate	1994–95	2
Thailand	Similan-class support ship	1996	1
Thailand	T-311 fire control radar	1991–92	25
Thailand	T-341 fire control radar	1991–92	4
Thailand	T-59 main battle tank	1985–87	60
Thailand	T-59-1 130mm towed gun	1985–88	54
Thailand	T-69 main battle tank	1987, 1989–92	503
Thailand	T-81 122mm MRL	1988	36
Thailand	T-85 130mm MRL	1988–89	60
Thailand	Type 531 APC	1987, 1989, 1991	492
Thailand	Type 69 Spaag AAV(G) (gun-armed)	1989–90	55
Thailand	Type 81 122mm MRL	1988	36
Thailand	Type 83 130mm MRL	1988–89	20
Thailand	YW-531 APC	1987, 1990–91	770
USA[a]	F-4 fighter	1988–89	6
USA	F-6 fighter	1988–89	6
USA	F-7 fighter	1988–89	12
Zimbabwe	F-6 fighter	1987	15
Zimbabwe	F-7 fighter	1983, 85–87, 89	52
Zimbabwe	T-59 main battle tank	1985–86	35
Zimbabwe	T-60 light tank	1984	20
Zimbabwe	Y-12 transport aircraft	1991	1

SOURCES: Bates Gill, "Chinese Military Modernization and Arms Proliferation in the Asia Pacific" (1998) and Stockholm International Peace Research Institute, *SIPRI Yearbook* (1983 through 1997). Some calculations are based on imputed averages. Where two figures were available for the same period, the lower was chosen.

[a]The United States purchased arms from China for training purposes.

BIBLIOGRAPHY

"A New China Embracing Nuclear Nonproliferation," *International Herald Tribune*, December 11, 1997, p. 1.

"Allies in Isolation: Burma and China Move Closer," *Jane's Defence Weekly*, September 15, 1990, p. 475.

Arnett, Eric, "Military Research and Development," in Stockholm International Peace Research Institute, *SIPRI Yearbook 1997: Armaments, Disarmament, and International Security*, Oxford University Press, Oxford, New York, 1997, pp. 211–238.

Arnett, Eric, "Military Technology: The Case of China," in Stockholm International Peace Research Institute, *SIPRI Yearbook 1995: Armaments, Disarmament, and International Security*, Oxford University Press, Oxford, New York, 1995, pp. 359–386.

"Birth of an Arms Salesman," *The Economist*, November 17, 1984, p. 40.

Bitzinger, Richard A., "Arms to Go: Chinese Arms Sales to the Third World," *International Security*, Vol. 17, No. 2, Fall 1992, pp. 84–111.

Bonavia, David, "Cheap and Deadly," *Far Eastern Economic Review*, May 21, 1987, p. 33.

Buszynski, Leszek, "New Aspirations and Old Constraints in Thailand's Military Policy," *Asian Survey*, Vol. 29, No. 11, November 1989, pp. 1057–1072.

Chanda, Nayan, "Technology Cocooned," *Far Eastern Economic Review*, November 5, 1987, p. 34.

Chao Ching-tseng, Pan Chu-sheng, and Liu Hua-ch'iu, "Analysis of Situation in World Arms Control, Disarmament," *Hsien-tai Chun-shih* (*Conmilit*), No. 230, March 6, 1996, pp. 15–16 in *Foreign Broadcast Information Service, Daily Report: China*, March 6, 1996.

Cheung, Tai Ming, "Proliferation Is Good, and There's Money in It Too," *Far Eastern Economic Review*, June 2, 1988, pp. 26–27.

Cheung, Tai Ming, "Missile Refrain," *Far Eastern Economic Review*, June 27, 1991, pp. 12–13.

"China Clamps Down on Its CW Trading," *Jane's Defense Weekly,* January 7, 1998, p. 5.

"China's Broken Promises," *Economist*, July 8, 1995, pp. 17–18.

Cordesman, Anthony H., and Ahmed S. Hashim, *Iraq: Sanctions and Beyond*, Westview, Boulder, CO, 1997.

Crispin, Shawn W., "Heading for a Fall," *Far Eastern Economic Review*, August 27, 1998, pp. 57–58.

Davis, Lynn, Under Secretary of State, U.S. Congress, House International Relations Committee Hearing, *Review of the Clinton Administration Nonproliferation Policy*, 104th Congress, 2nd Session, June 19, 1995.

Davis, Zachary S., "China's Nonproliferation and Export Control Policies," *Asian Survey*, Vol. 35, No. 6, June 1995, pp. 587–603.

Eikenberry, Karl W., *Explaining and Influencing Chinese Arms Transfers*, McNair Paper 36, Institute for National Strategic Studies, National Defense University, Washington DC, 1995.

Friedman, Norman, "Chinese Military Capacity: Industrial and Operational Weaknesses," in Eric Arnett (ed.), *Military Capacity and the Risk of War: China, India, Pakistan, and Iran*, Oxford University Press, New York, 1997, pp. 61–75.

Friedman, Stephen, and Elizabeth Economy, *Managing the Taiwan Issue: Key Is Better U.S. Relations with China*, Council on Foreign Relations, New York, 1995.

Frieman, Wendy, "China's Defense Industries," *The Pacific Review*, Vol. 6, No. 1, pp. 51–62.

Gaffney, Frank J., "China Arms the Rogues," *Middle East Quarterly*, September 1997, pp. 33–39.

Garver, John W., "China-India Rivalry in Nepal: The Clash Over Chinese Arms Sales," *Asian Survey*, Vol. 31, No. 10, October 1991, pp. 956–975.

Gertz, Bill, "Nuclear Sales to China Too Chancy, Foes Insist," *Washington Times*, October 28, 1997, p. 1.

Gertz, Bill, "Beijing Flouts Nuke-Sales Ban," *Washington Times*, October 9, 1996, p. A1.

Gill, R. Bates, "China Looks to Thailand: Exporting Arms, Exporting Influence," *Asian Survey*, Vol. 31, No. 6, June 1991, pp. 526–539.

Gill, R. Bates, *Chinese Arms Transfers: Purposes, Patterns, and Prospects in the New World Order*, Praeger, Westport, CT, 1992.

Gill, R. Bates, "Curbing Beijing's Arms Sales," *Orbis*, Summer 1992, pp. 379–396.

Gill, Bates, *Silkworms and Summitry: Chinese Arms Exports to Iran and U.S.-China Relations*, The Asia and Pacific Rim Institute of the American Jewish Committee, New York, 1997.

Gill, Bates, "Chinese Military Modernization and Arms Proliferation in the Asia-Pacific," in Jonathan D. Pollack and Richard H. Yang (eds.), *In China's Shadow: Regional Perspectives on Chinese Foreign Policy and Military Development*, RAND, 1998, pp. 10–36.

Godemont, Francois, "China's Arms Sales," in Gerald Segal and Richard H. Yang (eds.), *Chinese Economic Reform: The Impact on Security*, Routledge, London and New York, 1996, pp. 95–110.

Hyer, Eric, "China's Arms Merchants: Profits in Command," *The China Quarterly*, No. 132, December 1992, pp. 1101–1118.

International Institute for Strategic Studies, *The Military Balance, 1997/98*, Oxford University Press, London, 1997.

International Monetary Fund, *Direction of Trade Statistics*, March 1998.

Kan, Shirley A., *China's Compliance with International Arms Control Agreements,* CRS Report to Congress, Washington DC, Congressional Research Service, updated January 16, 1998.

Kan, Shirley A., *Chinese Proliferation of Weapons of Mass Destruction: Background and Analysis*, CRS Report for Congress, Congressional Research Service, Washington DC, September 13, 1996.

Kan, Shirley A., *Chinese Proliferation of Weapons of Mass Destruction: Current Policy Issues*, CRS Issue Brief, Congressional Research Service, Washington DC, March 23, 1998.

Karniol, Robert, "China Supplied Iran with Decontamination Agent," *Jane's Defense Weekly*, April 30, 1997, p. 17.

Karniol, Robert, "China's $4.5b Deal with Iran Cools as Funds Fail," *Jane's Defense Weekly*, August 6, 1997, p. 14.

Kemp, Geoffrey, *The Control of the Middle East Arms Race*, Carnegie Endowment for International Peace, Washington, DC, 1991.

Lawrence, Susan V., "Sparring Partners," *Far Eastern Economic Review*, July 9, 1998, pp. 12–14.

Lennon, Alexander T., "Trading Guns, Not Butter," *The China Business Review*, March–April 1994, pp. 47–49.

Lennox, Duncan (ed.), *Jane's Strategic Weapons Systems*, Issue 18, May 1995.

Lewis, John W., Hua Di, and Xue Litai, "Beijing's Defense Establishment: Solving the Arms-Export Enigma," *International Security*, Vol. 15, No. 4, Spring 1991, pp. 87–109.

Lintner, Bertil, "Rangoon's Rubicon," *Far Eastern Economic Review*, February 11, 1993, p. 28.

Lintner, Bertil, "Arms for Eyes," *Far Eastern Economic Review*, December 16, 1993, p. 26.

Lintner, Bertil, "Burma Road," *Far Eastern Economic Review*, November 6, 1997, pp. 16–17.

Lintner, Bertil, ". . . But Stay on Guard," *Far Eastern Economic Review*, July 16, 1998, p. 21.

Mack, Andrew, *Proliferation in Northeast Asia*, Henry L. Stimson Center, Washington DC, 1996.

Mullins, Robert E., "The Dynamics of Chinese Missile Proliferation," *The Pacific Review*, Vol. 8, No. 1, 1995, pp. 137–157.

Mulvenon, James, *Soldiers of Fortune*, Ph.D. Dissertation, University of California at Los Angeles, 1998.

Office of the Secretary of Defense, *Proliferation: Threat and Response*, Washington DC, November 1997.

Pan Guang, "China's Success in the Middle East," *Middle East Quarterly*, Vol. 4, No. 4, December 1997.

Pincus, Walter, "Iran May Soon Gain Missile Capability," *Washington Post*, July 24, 1998, p. A28.

"Prices and Trends," *Far Eastern Economic Review*, August 27, 1998, p. 66.

"Row Over?" *Economist*, May 18, 1996, pp. 37–38.

Sisimandis, Roxane D.V., "The Paradoxes of Asian Security," *The China Business Review*, November–December 1995, pp. 9–13.

Smith, R. Jeffrey, "China Linked to Pakistani Missile Plant: Secret Project Could Renew Sanctions Issue," *Washington Post*, August 25, 1996, p. A1.

Sneider, Daniel, "China's Arms Bazaar," *Far Eastern Economic Review*, December 18, 1996, p. 23.

Sricharatchanya, Paisal, "'Friendship' Arms Sales," *Far Eastern Economic Review*, March 19, 1987, pp. 15–16.

Sricharatchanya, Paisal, "The Chinese Firecracker," *Far Eastern Economic Review*, December 8, 1988, p. 34.

State Council of the People's Republic of China, "China: Arms Control and Disarmament," *Beijing Review*, November 27–December 3, 1995, pp. 10–25.

State Council of the People's Republic of China, "China's National Defense," *Beijing Review*, August 10–16, 1998, pp. 12–34.

Stockholm International Peace Research Institute, *SIPRI Yearbook,* 1983–1997 editions, Oxford University Press, Oxford, New York, 1983–1997.

Tasker, Rodney, "Order Arms," *Far Eastern Economic Review*, October 4, 1990, p. 20.

U.S. Congress, Senate Governmental Affairs Subcommittee on International Security, Proliferation, and Federal Services, *The Proliferation Primer,* Washington DC, 1998.

U.S. Congress, Senate Governmental Affairs Subcommittee on International Security, Proliferation, and Federal Services, *China: Proliferation Case Studies*, Hearing on April 10, 1997, 105th Congress, Session 1, 1997, p. 8.

Wallerstein, Mitchel B., "China and Proliferation: A Path Not Taken?" *Survival*, Vol. 38, No. 3, Autumn 1996, pp. 58–66.

"Who Us?" *Economist*, October 6, 1990, p. 38.

Wolfsthal, Jon Brook, "U.S. and Chinese Views on Proliferation: Trying to Bridge the Gap," *The Nonproliferation Review*, Fall 1994, pp. 60–64.

Woon, Eden Y., "Chinese Arms Sales and U.S.-China Military Relations," *Asian Survey*, Vol. 29, No. 6, June 1989, pp. 601–618.